little
moments
of
love.

little moments of love

Catana Chetwynd

Andrews McMeel
PUBLISHING®

INTRODUCTION

Have you ever looked at your significant other and thought, "Wow, we have a weird relationship. If other people saw what we do, it would be odd and embarrassing"? Well, to be honest, that's what we thought, too, before the comics began.

It all started on Thanksgiving Day 2016 when John and I were chatting about the mere-exposure effect in psychology—the idea that encountering someone more increases their chances of liking you. John suggested that it would be a great premise for a comic: Me, following John around, trying to encounter him more.

Three hours and a Thanksgiving dinner later, the first Catana Comic had been created, and within a week, five more. The comics were intended for John's eyes only, but John was convinced that the Internet would love them. So with my timid approval, he posted them. We were instantly floored by the amount of support the comics received.

Who would've known how many odd, happy couples were just like us? We surely didn't know back then. But a little more than a year later, we are surrounded by them! We constantly feel overjoyed by our followers' love, positivity, and silliness. We love to read and hear everyone's kind comments and their own little jokes, see people tagging their significant others, and feel their blatantly overflowing love for their relationship.

Even though these comics were not in our life plan at all, they have become so important to us! We are just a happy little couple from Upstate New York (and when I say little, I mean John is six foot seven, so maybe little isn't quite accurate).

Our followers and fans are very important to us. Without you guys, we would not be writing this. Thank you to everyone who finds joy in Catana Comics—it warms our hearts to know that there are so many other couples out there fueled by love, silliness, ponytail beards, finger guns, and good ol' snugging. We hope you find yourselves in the pages of this book.

mere exposure effect:
Simply encountering someone more often increases
their chances of liking you

babe, we're already dating.

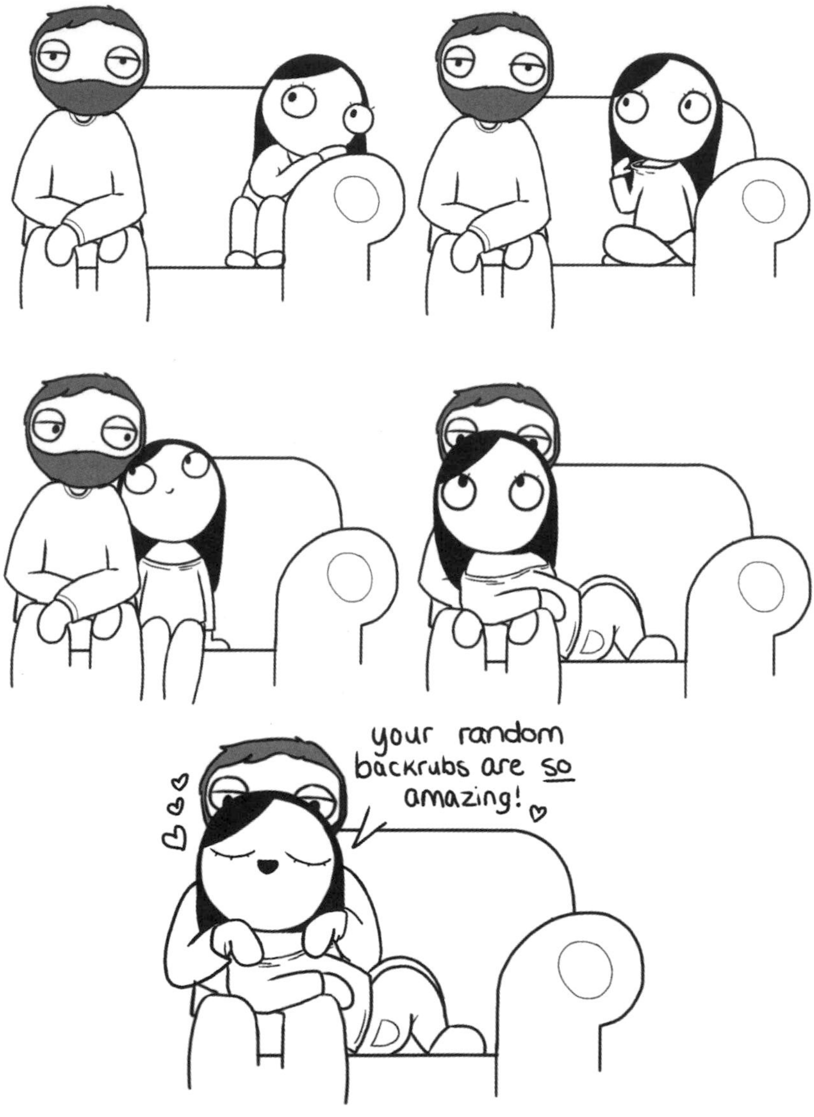
your random backrubs are so amazing!

So good to see you!
come on in!
We really came for you!

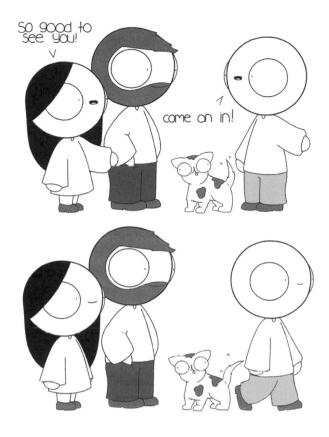

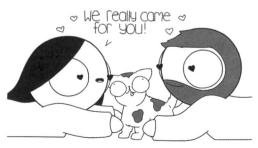

Signs your girlfriend wants attention

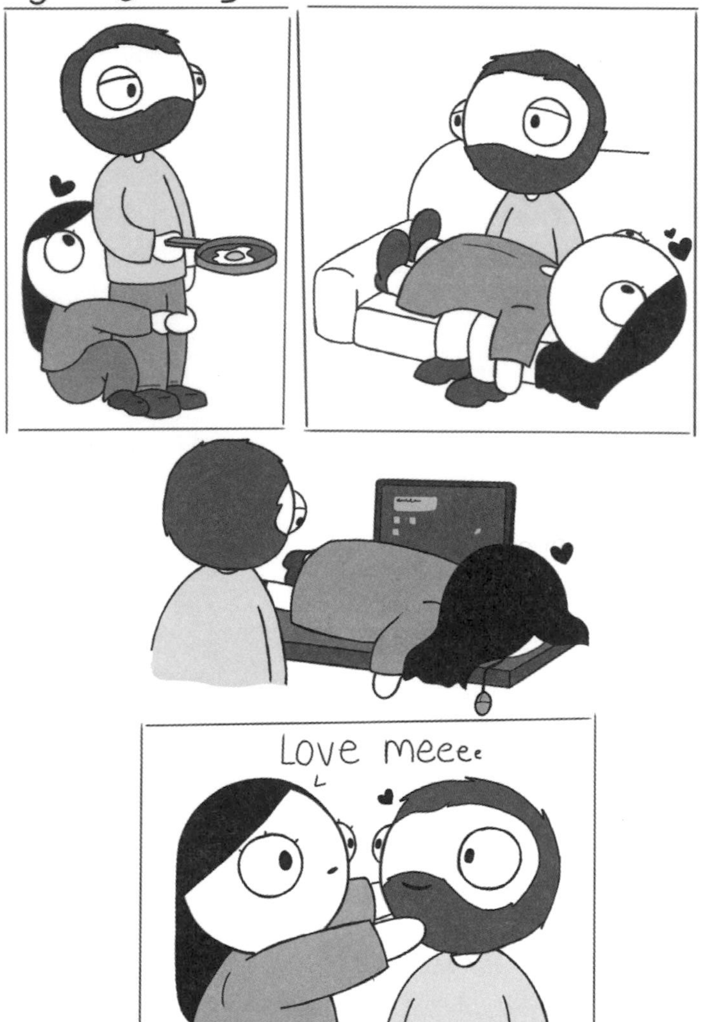
Love meeee

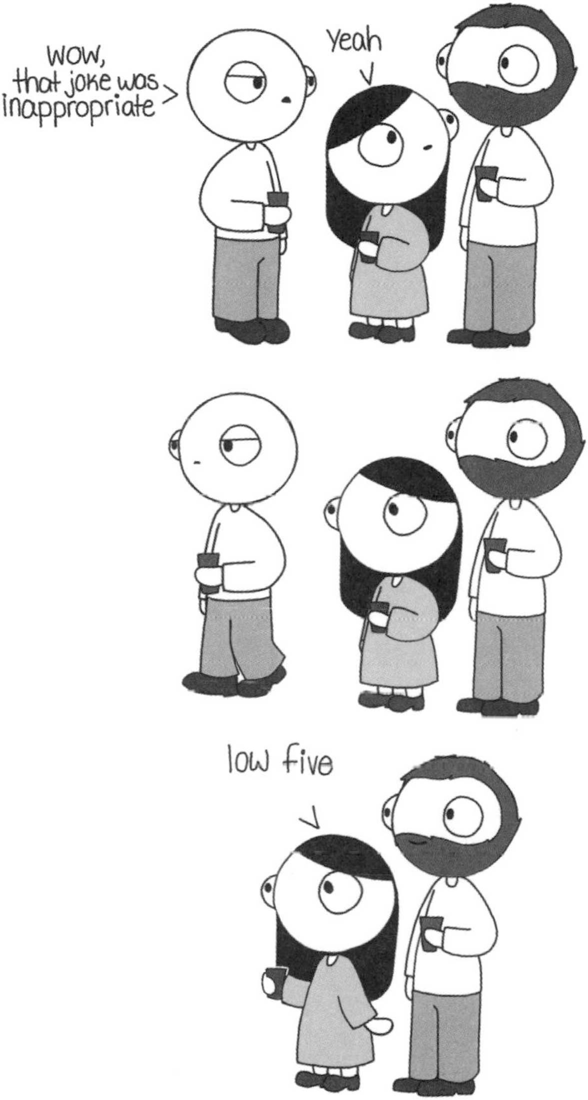
wow, that joke was inappropriate
yeah
low five

where do all my clothes keep going?
hey

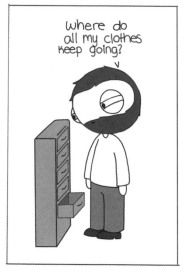

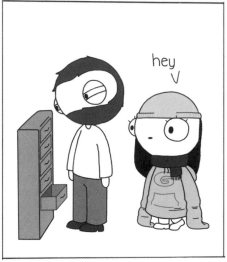

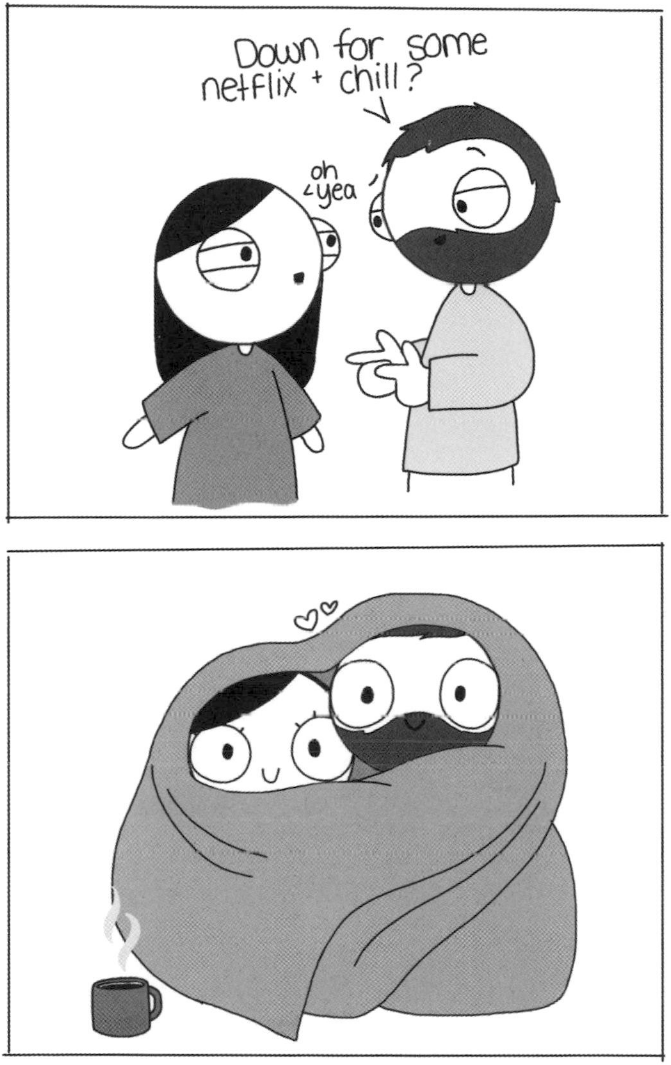
Down for some netflix + chill?
oh yea

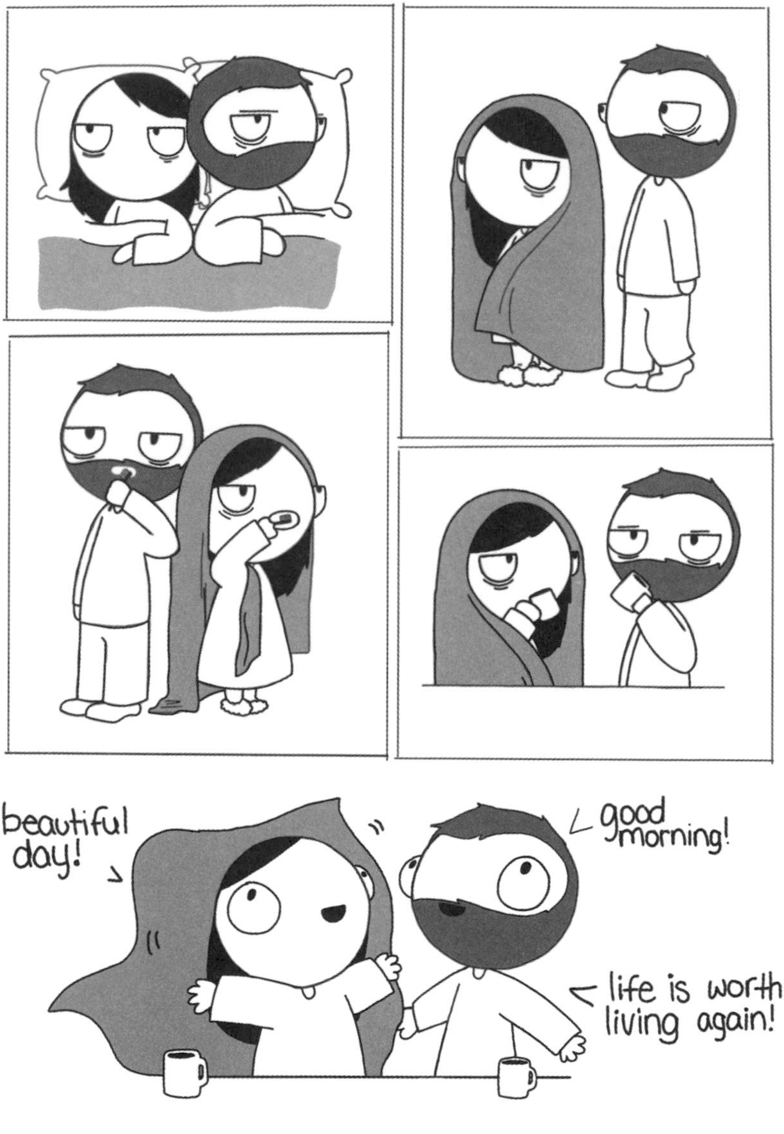
beautiful day!
good morning!
life is worth living again!

i'm going to touch your butt extra today.

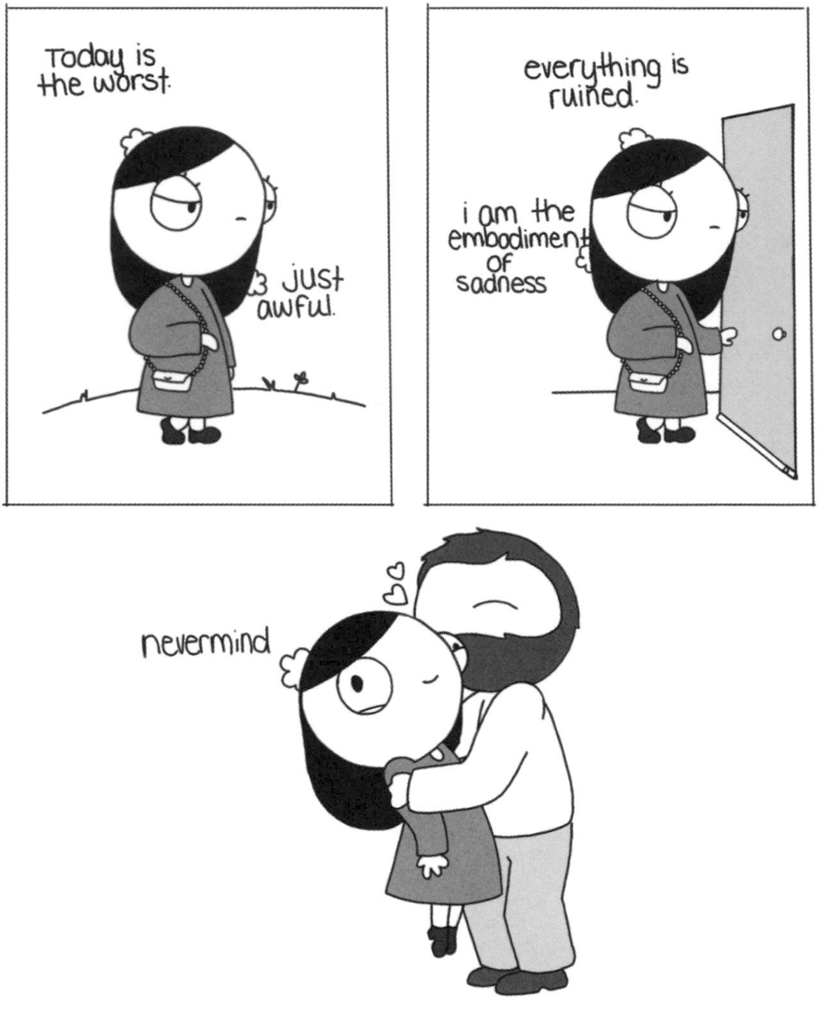
Today is the worst.
just awful.
everything is ruined.
i am the embodiment of sadness
nevermind

fridays

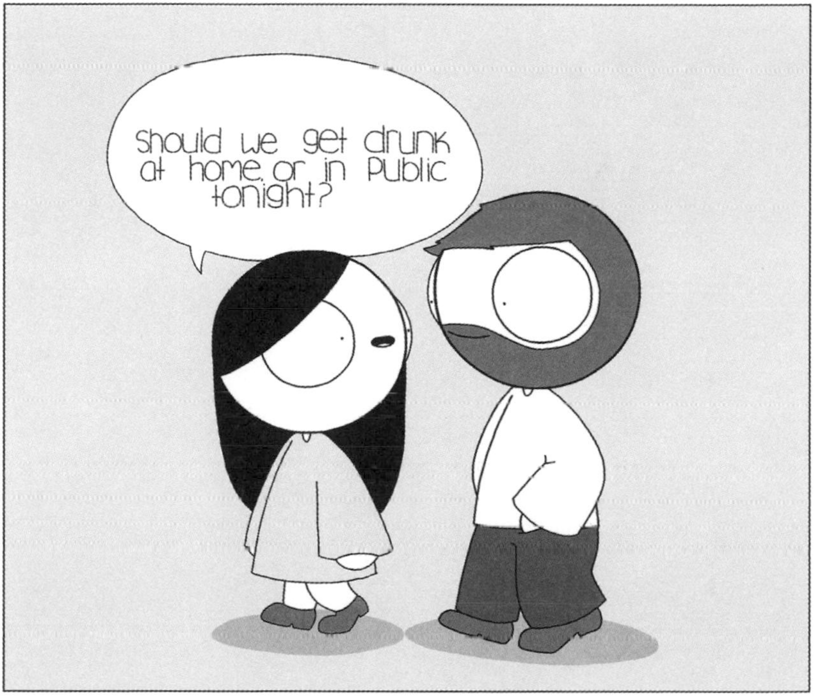
should we get drunk at home or in public tonight?

Trying To Be Romantic in Winter Clothes

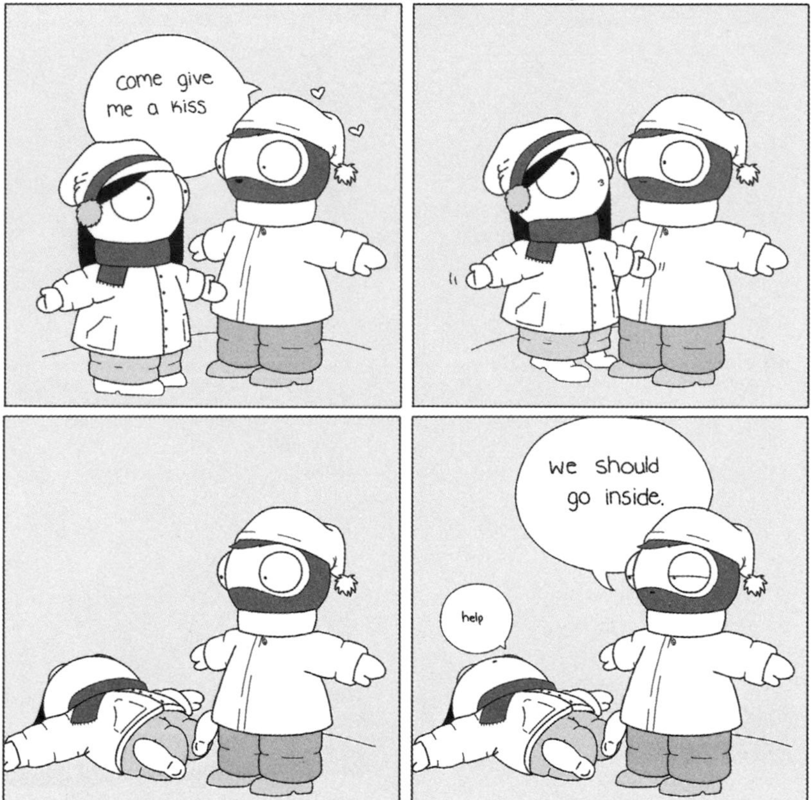
come give me a kiss
help
we should go inside.

Tall People

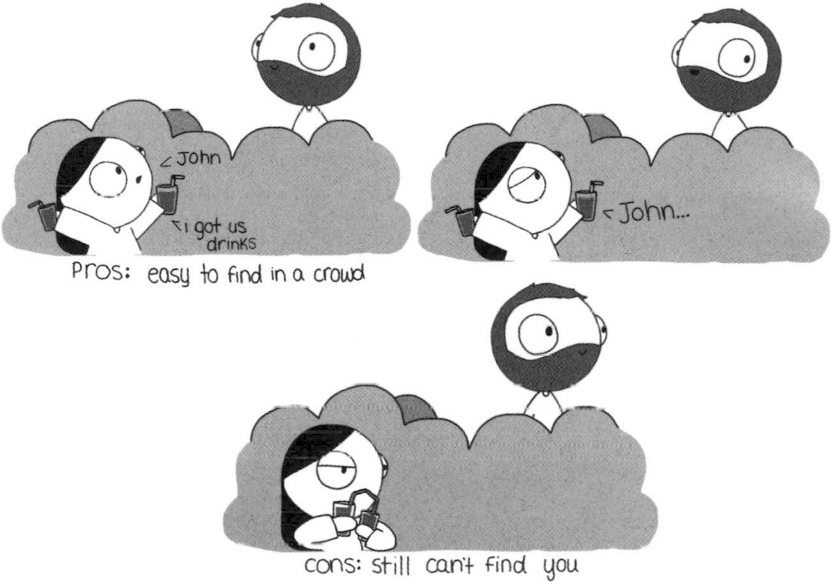

John
I got us drinks
Pros: easy to find in a crowd
John...
cons: still can't find you

Doing Nothing Alone Vs. Together

this is awful
this is amazing!

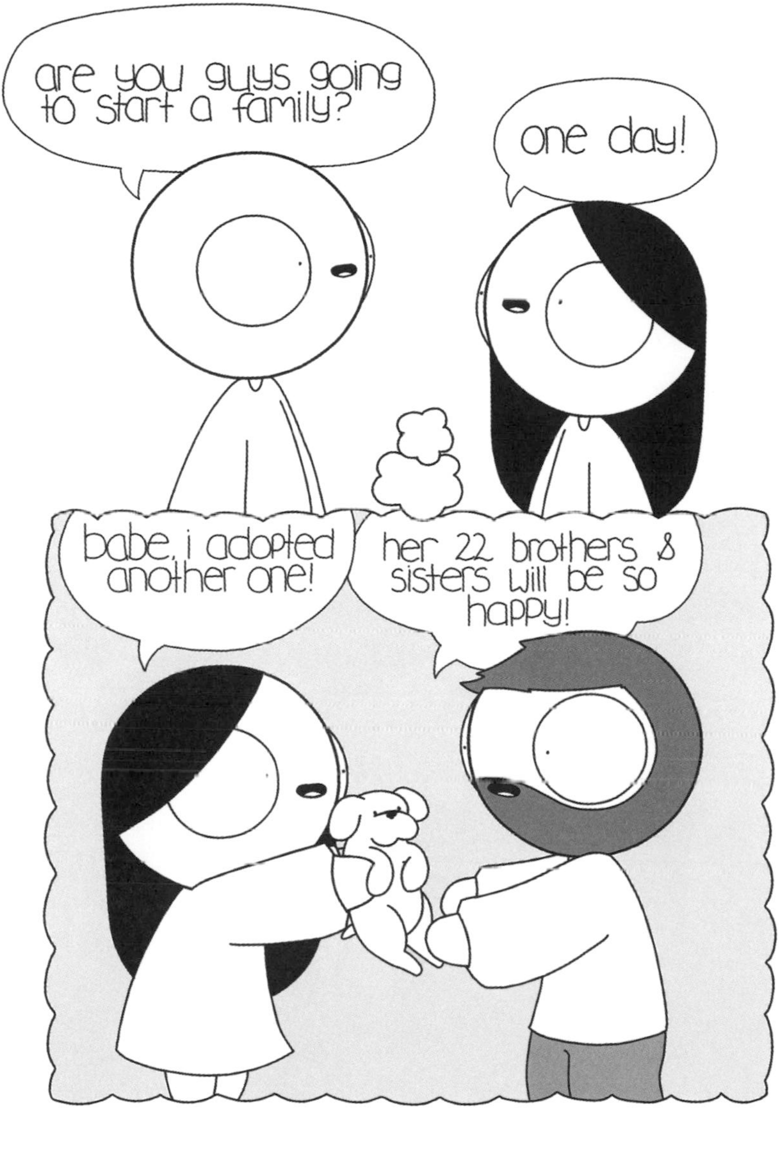
are you guys going to start a family?
one day!
babe, i adopted another one!
her 22 brothers & sisters will be so happy!

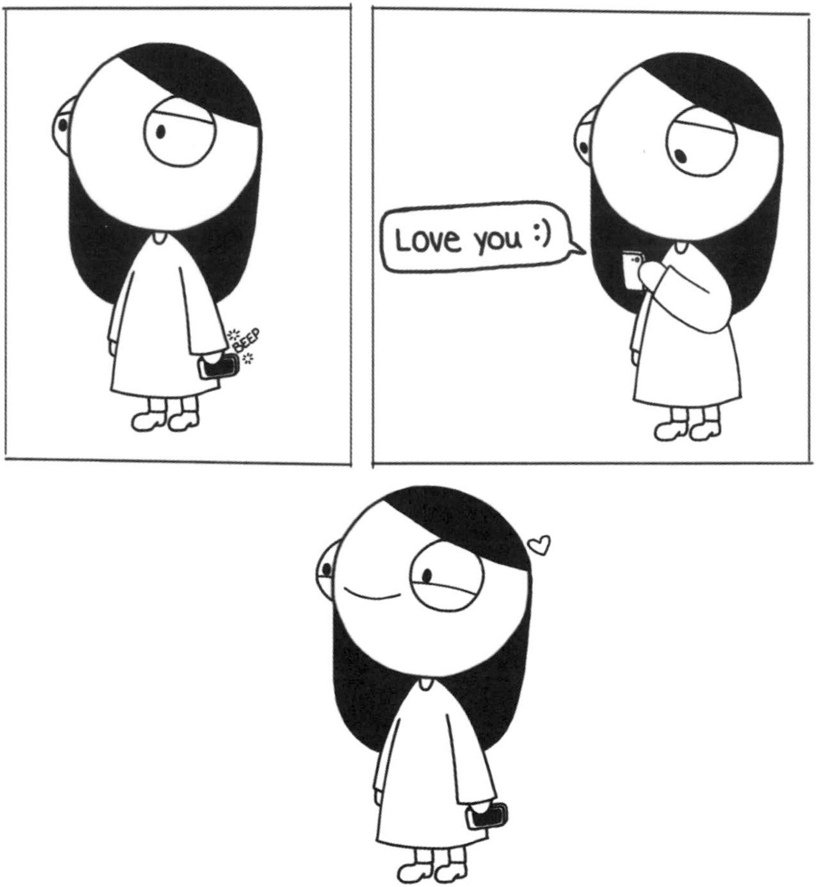
BEEP
Love you :)

Mornings

zzz
fresh
well rested
morning glow
good morning beautiful
none of those things
hi

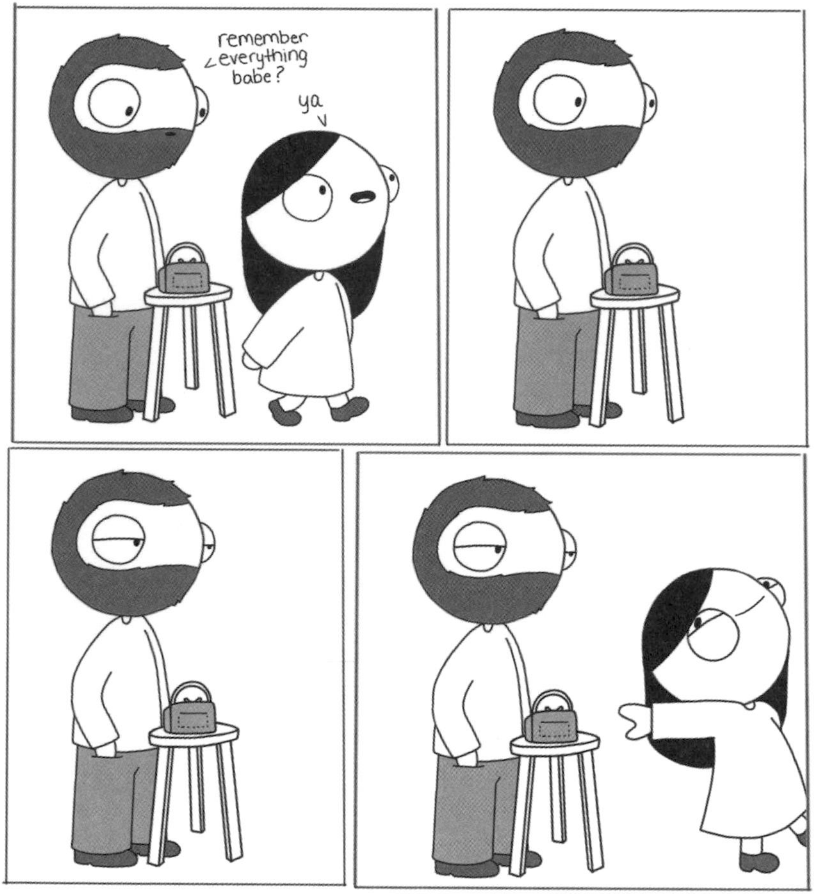
remember everything babe?
ya

When Someone's Checkin Out Babe A Little Too Hard

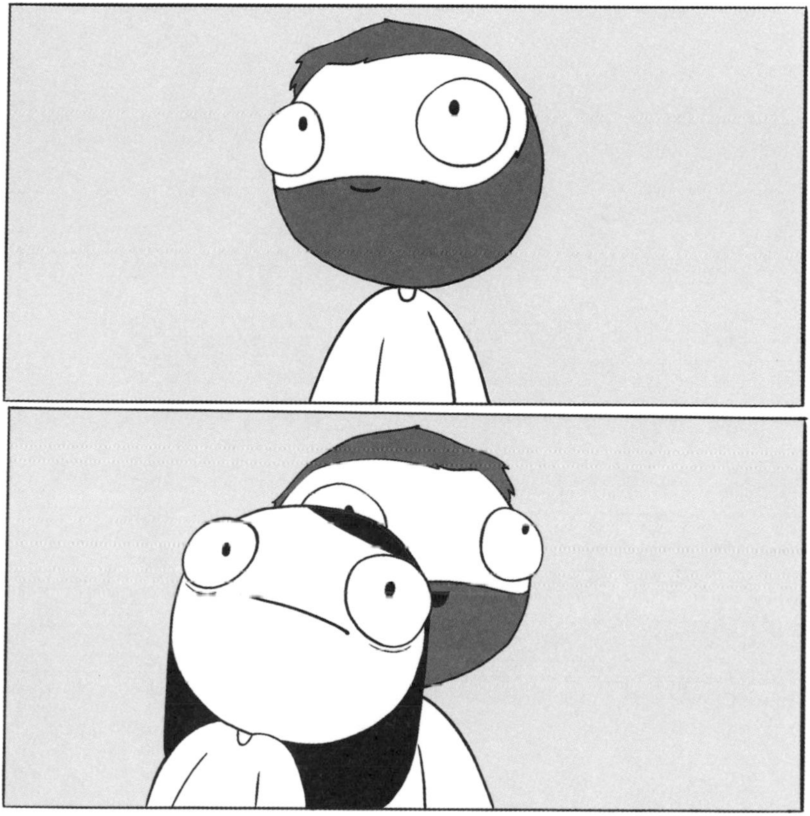

A Night Out in Heels

expectation

reality

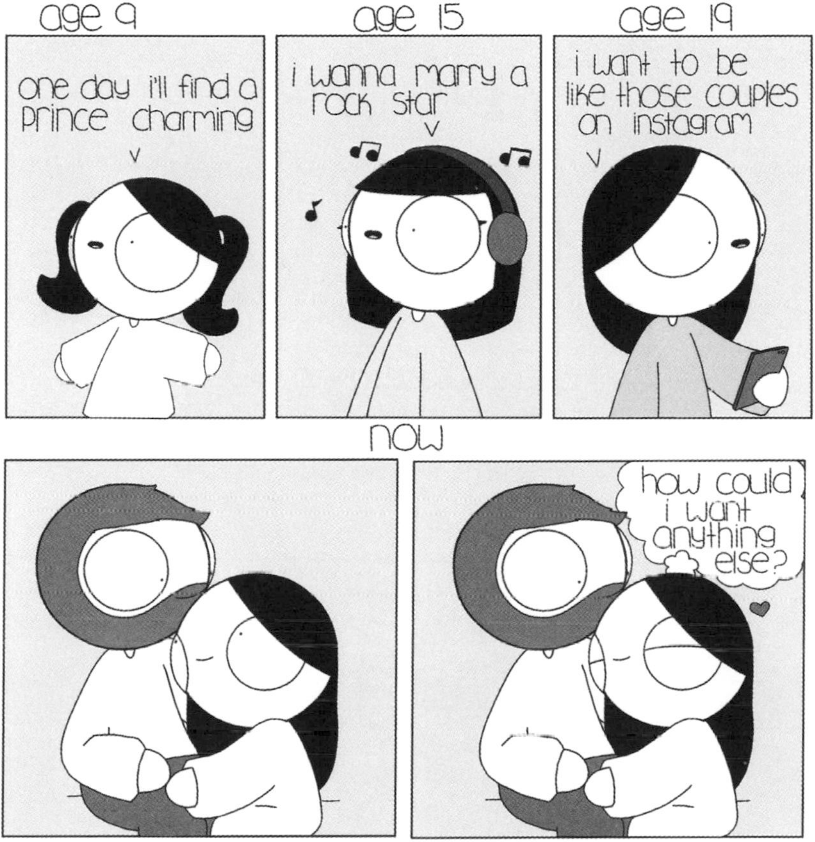
age 9
one day i'll find a prince charming
age 15
i wanna marry a rock star
age 19
i want to be like those couples on instagram
now
how could i want anything else?

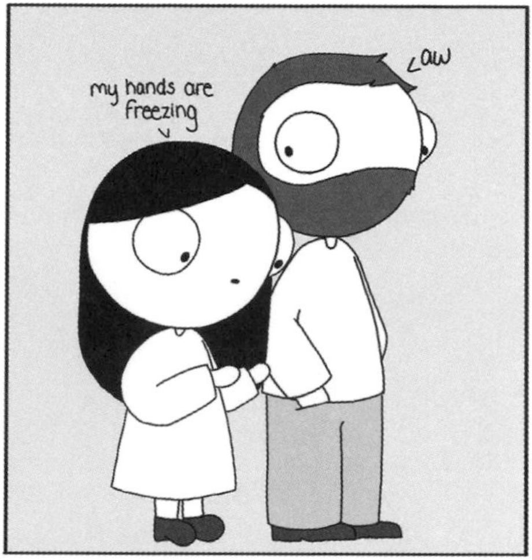
my hands are freezing
aw

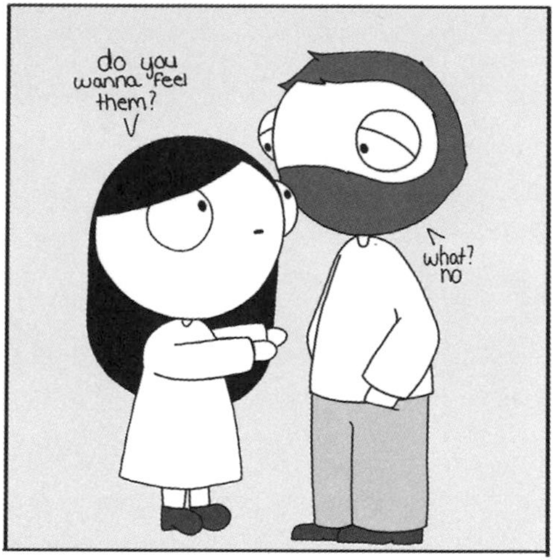
do you wanna feel them?
what? no

HAHAAAA
too bad

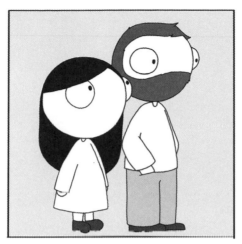

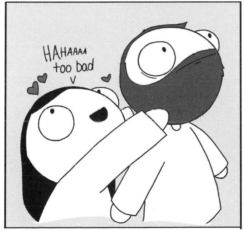

I GOT A ROOMBA
OH MY GOD
I'll Start her up
I'll get the googly eyes!

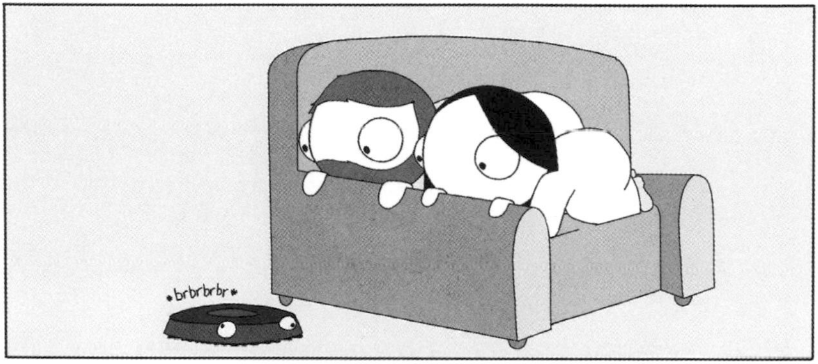
brbrbrbr

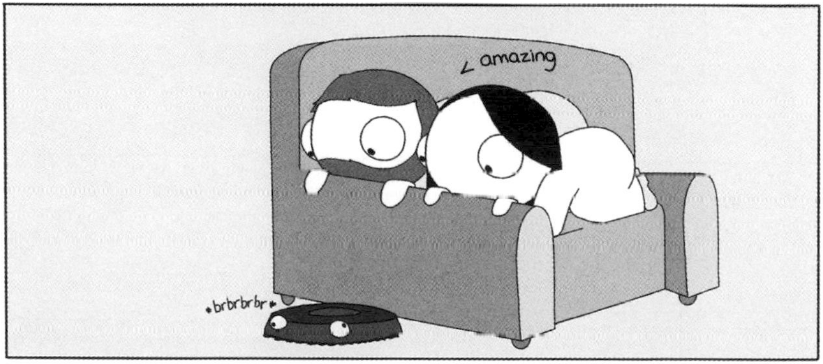
amazing
brbrbrbr

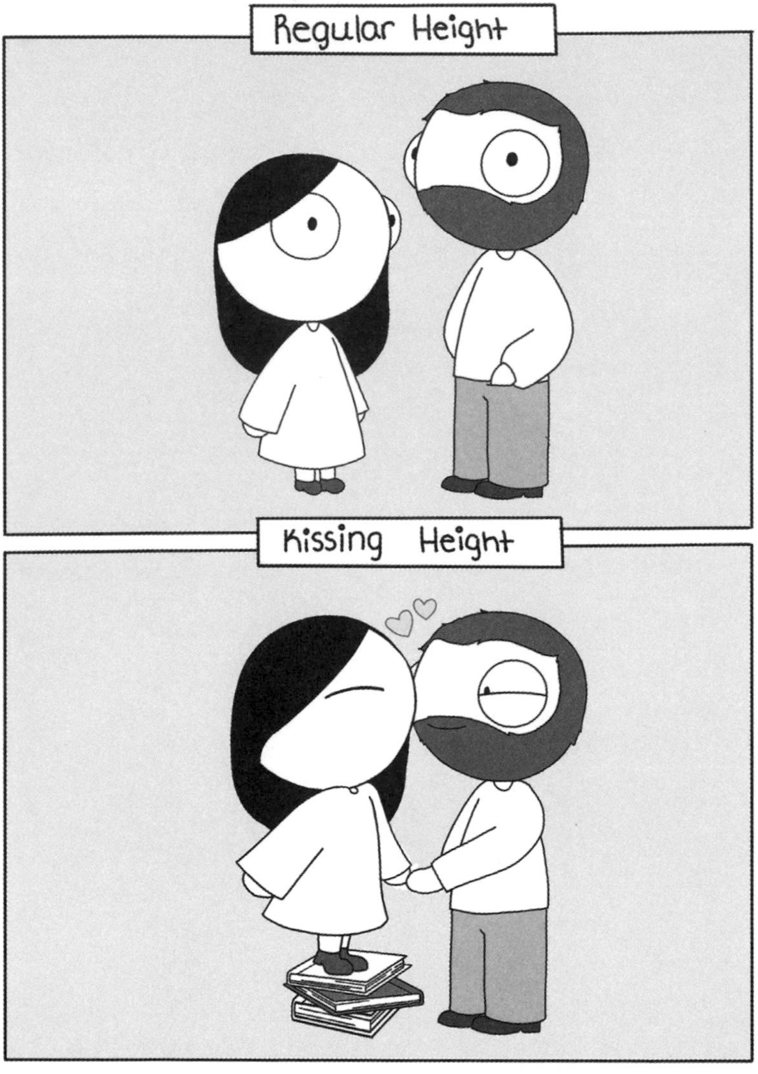
Regular Height
Kissing Height

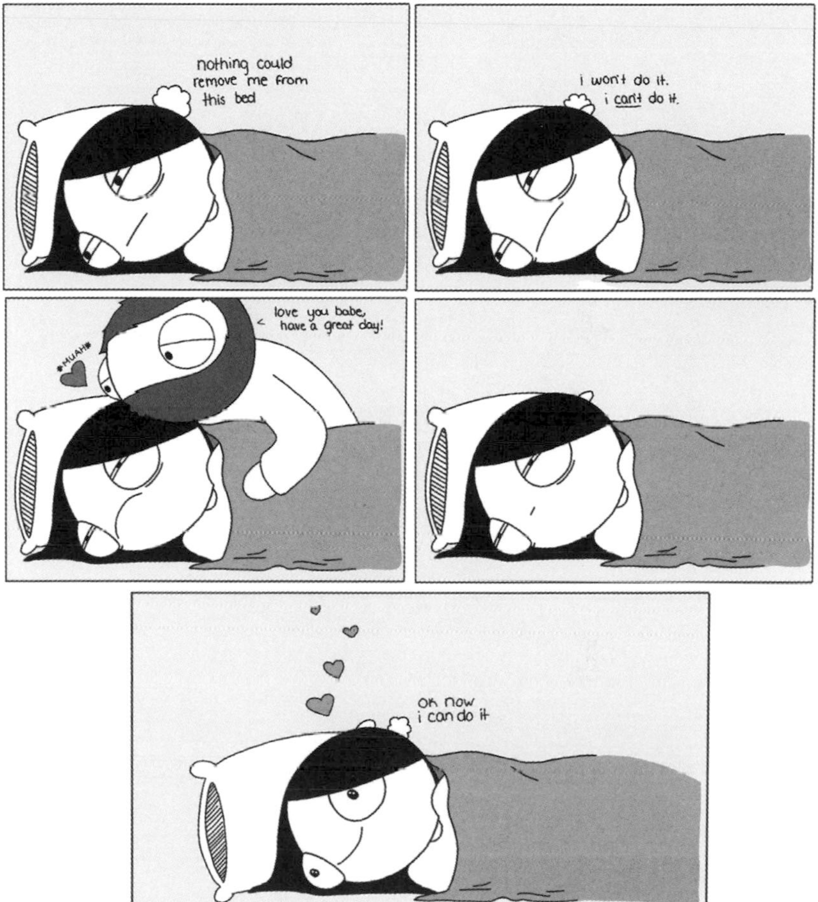
nothing could remove me from this bed
i won't do it.
i can't do it.
MUAH
love you babe, have a great day!
ok now i can do it

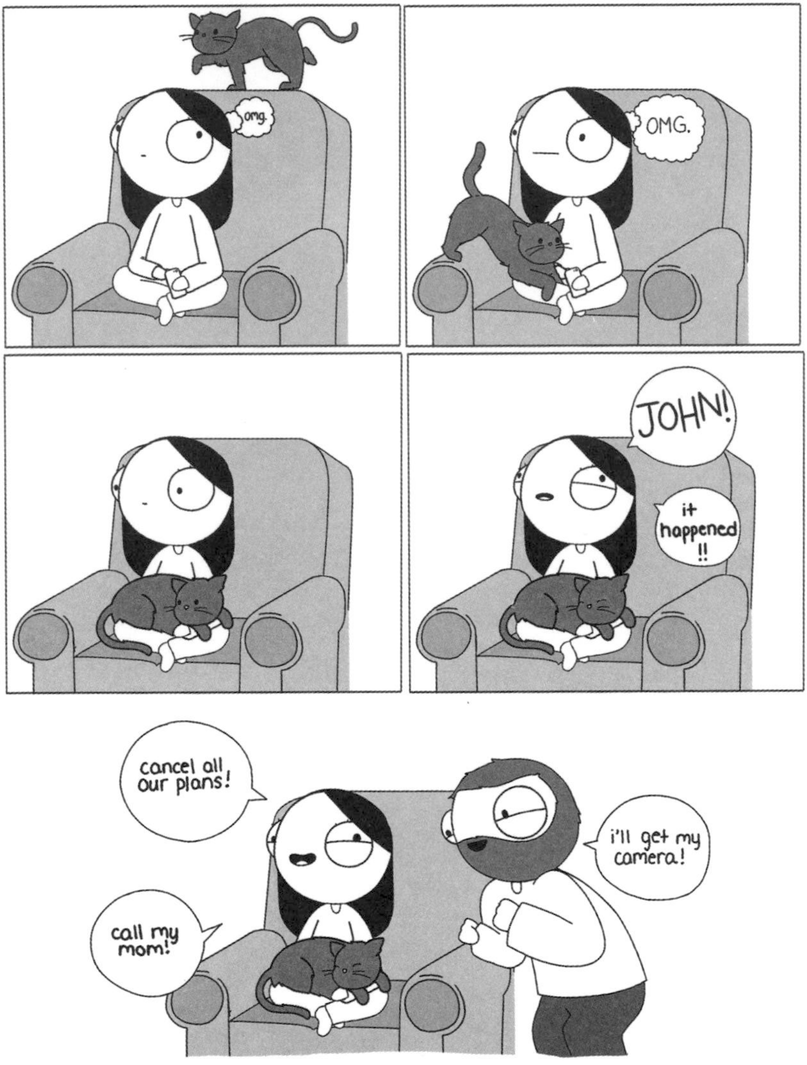
omg.
OMG.
JOHN!
it happened !!
cancel all our plans!
i'll get my camera!
call my mom!

Signs your girlfriend is a Cat

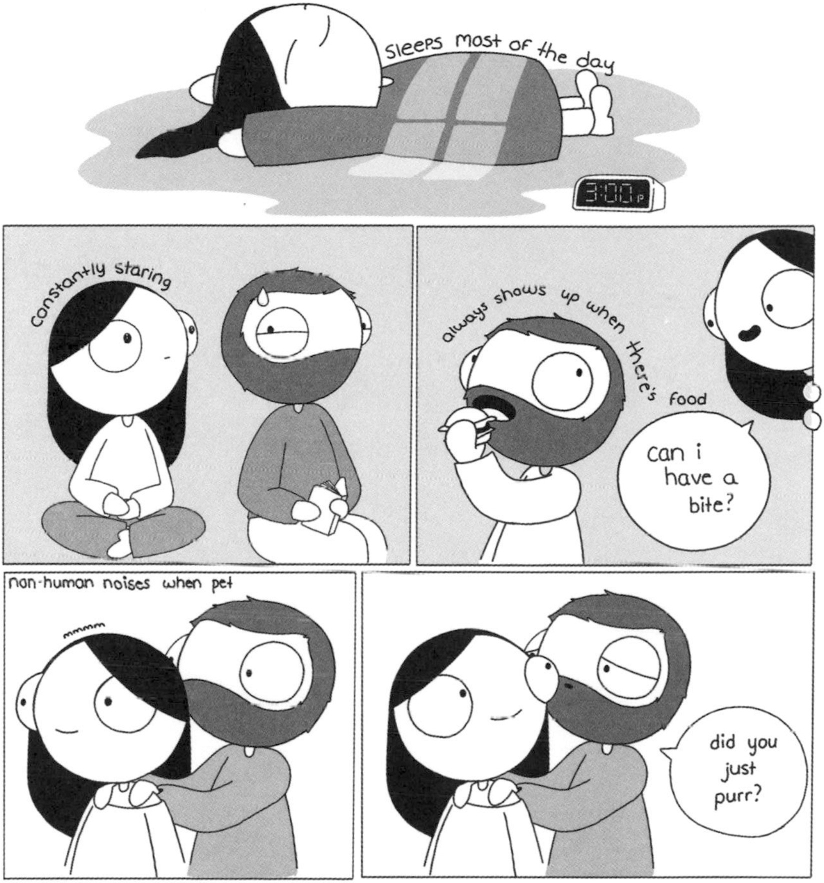
sleeps most of the day
3:00 P
constantly staring
always shows up when there's food
can i have a bite?
non-human noises when pet
mmmm
did you just purr?

When i'm Sick

you still wanna go to that thing tonight?
yea
it's just a little pneumonia

When he's Sick

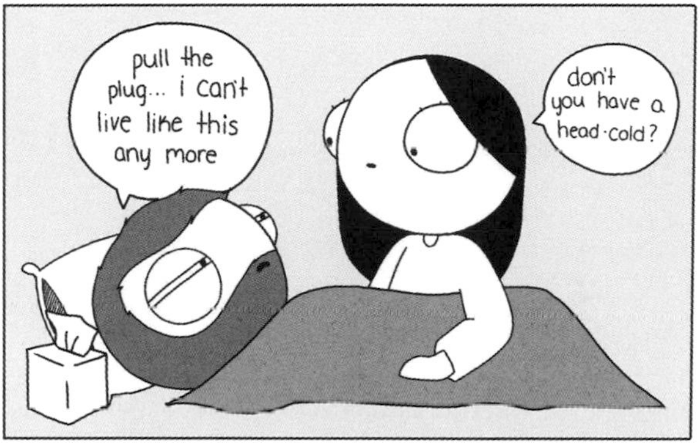
pull the plug... i can't live like this any more
don't you have a head-cold?

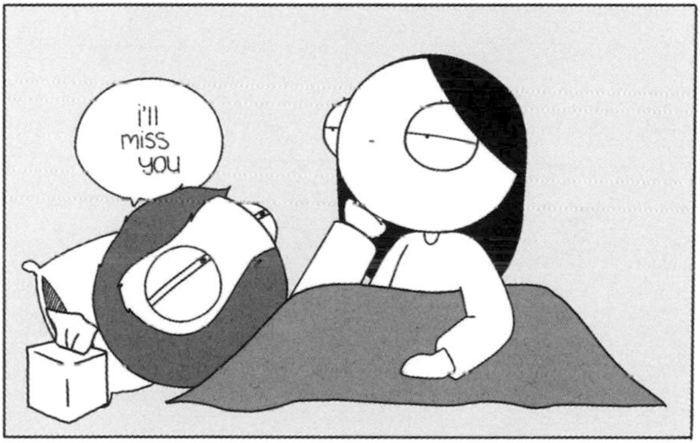
i'll miss you

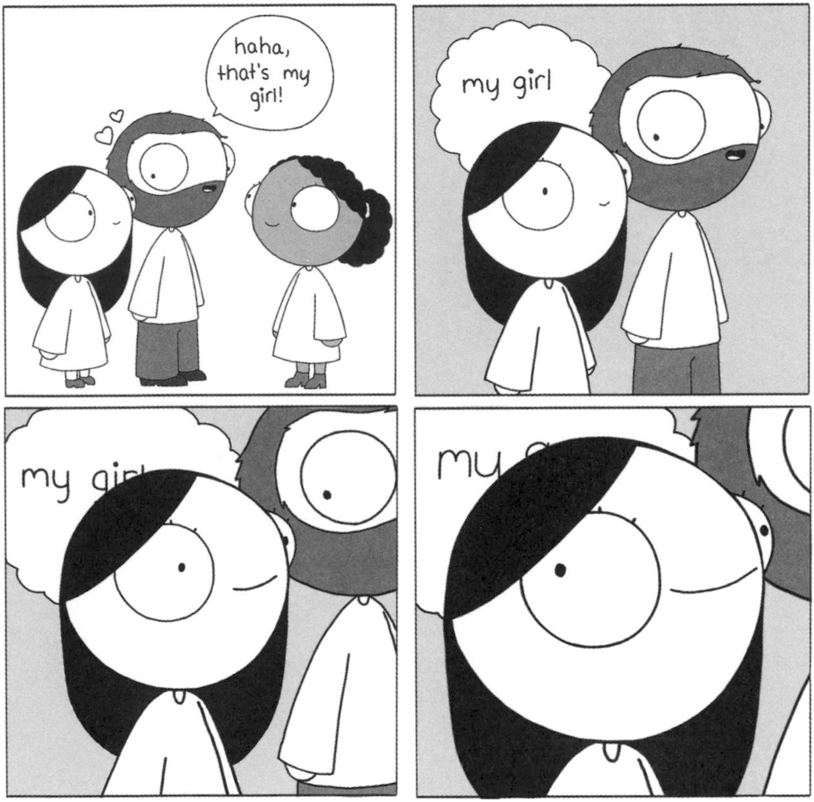
haha, that's my girl!
my girl
my gir
my

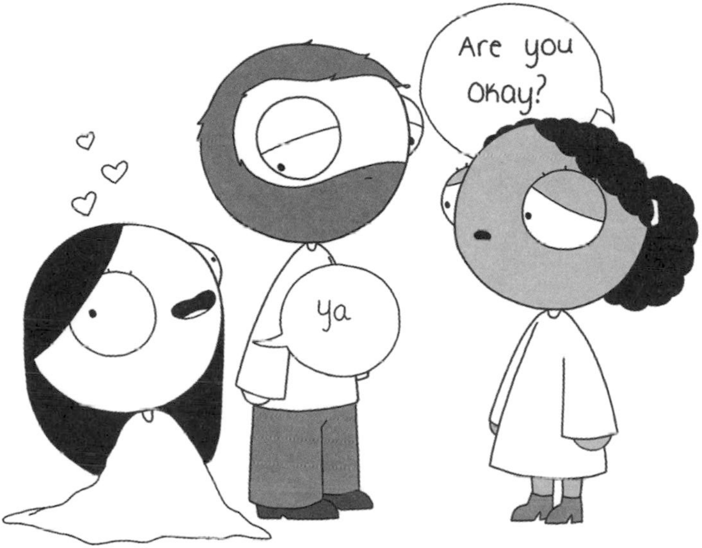
Are you Okay?
ya

When She's Really Into Facial Hair

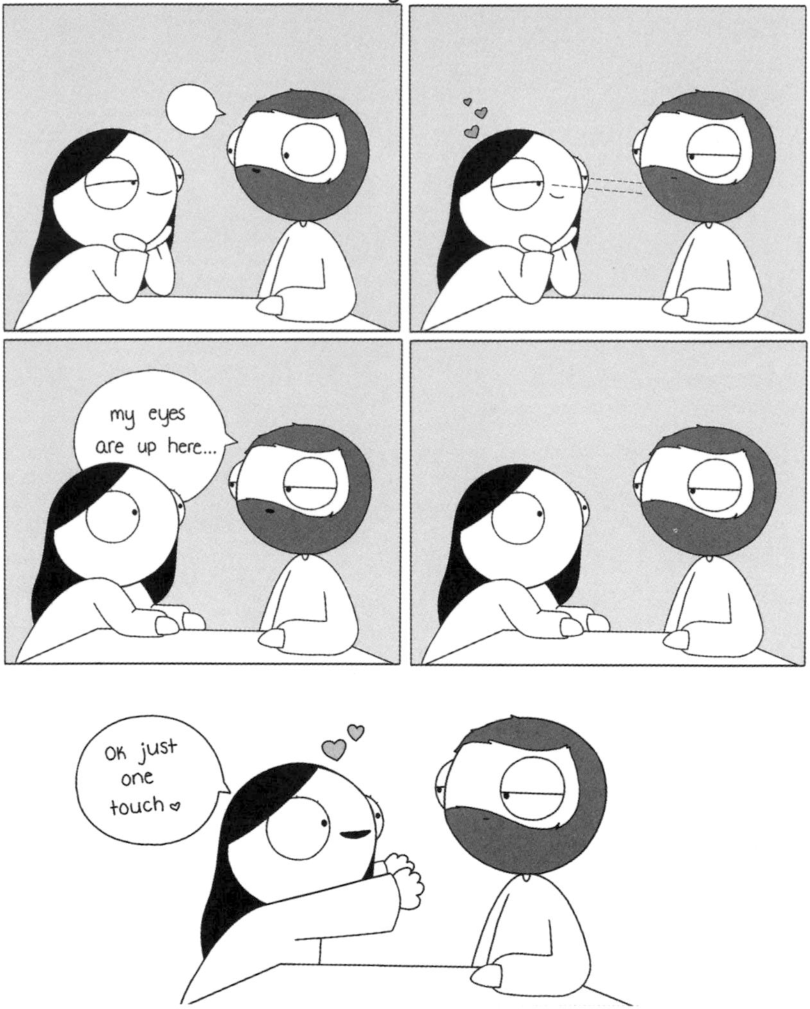
my eyes are up here...
ok just one touch ♡

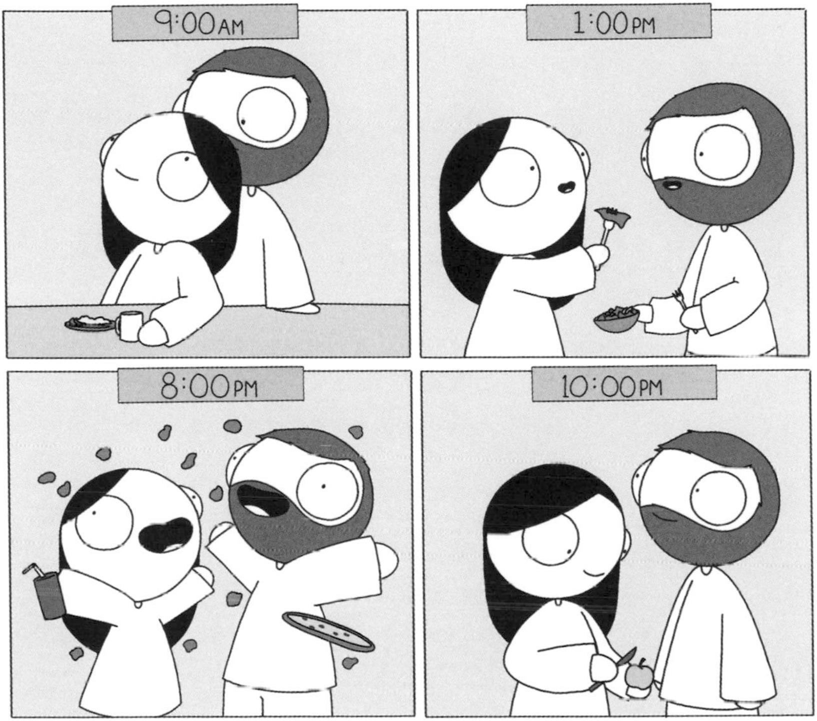
9:00AM
1:00PM
8:00PM
10:00PM

Rough day.
would a burrito help?
yea...

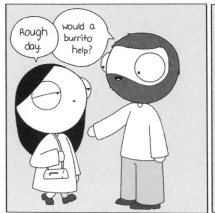

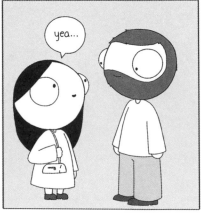

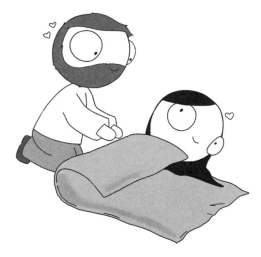

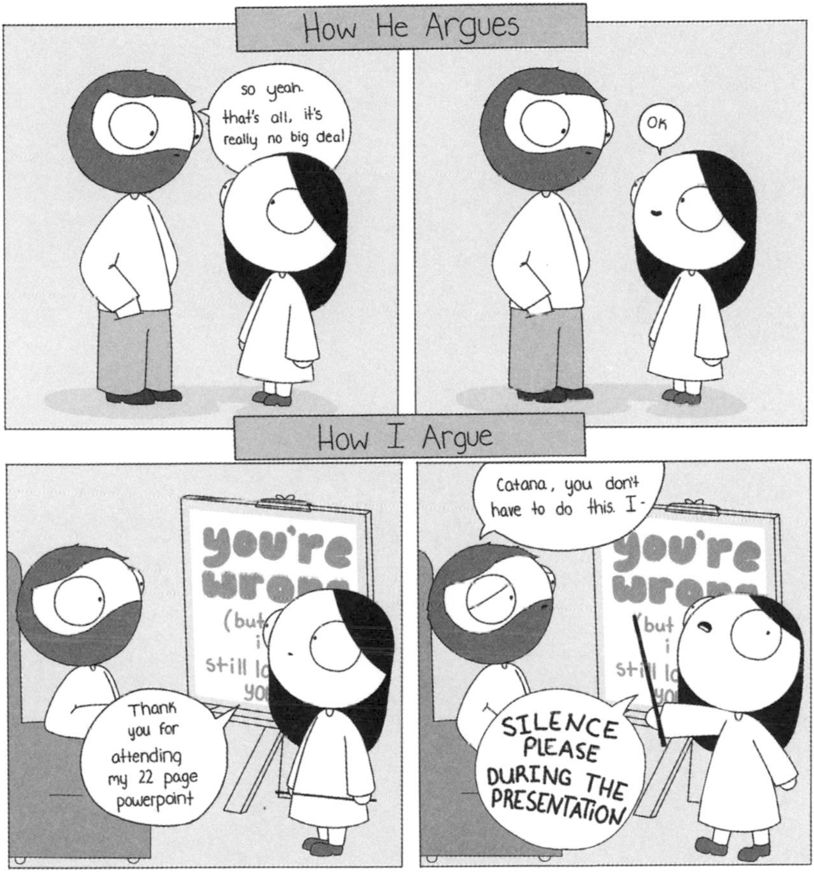
How He Argues
so yeah. that's all, it's really no big deal
OK
How I Argue
you're
Thank you for attending my 22 page powerpoint
Catana, you don't have to do this. I-
SILENCE PLEASE DURING THE PRESENTATION

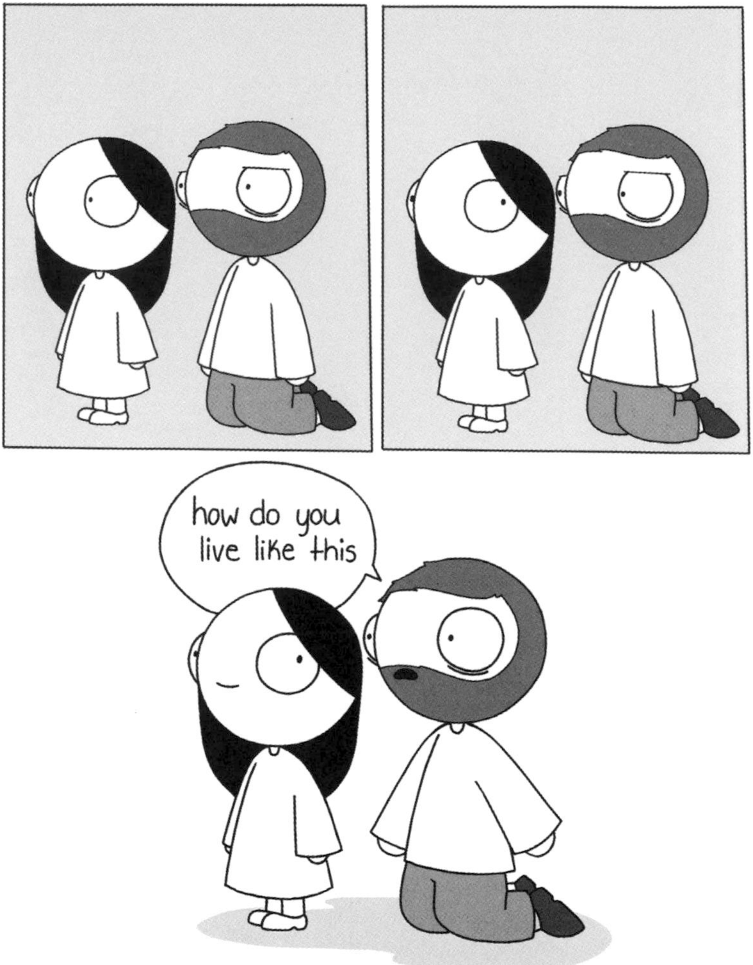
how do you live like this

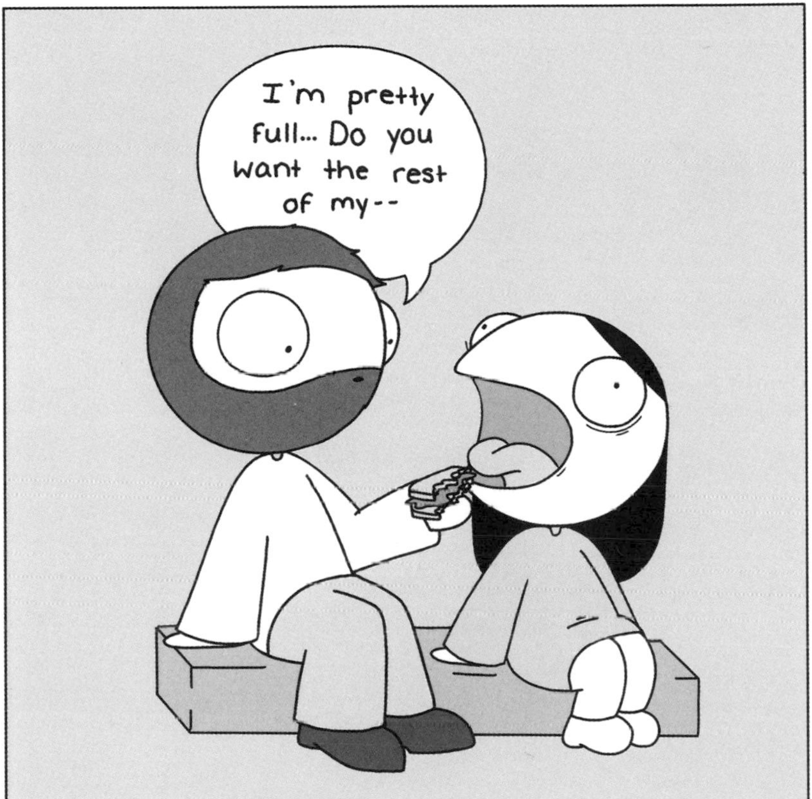
I'm pretty full... Do you want the rest of my--

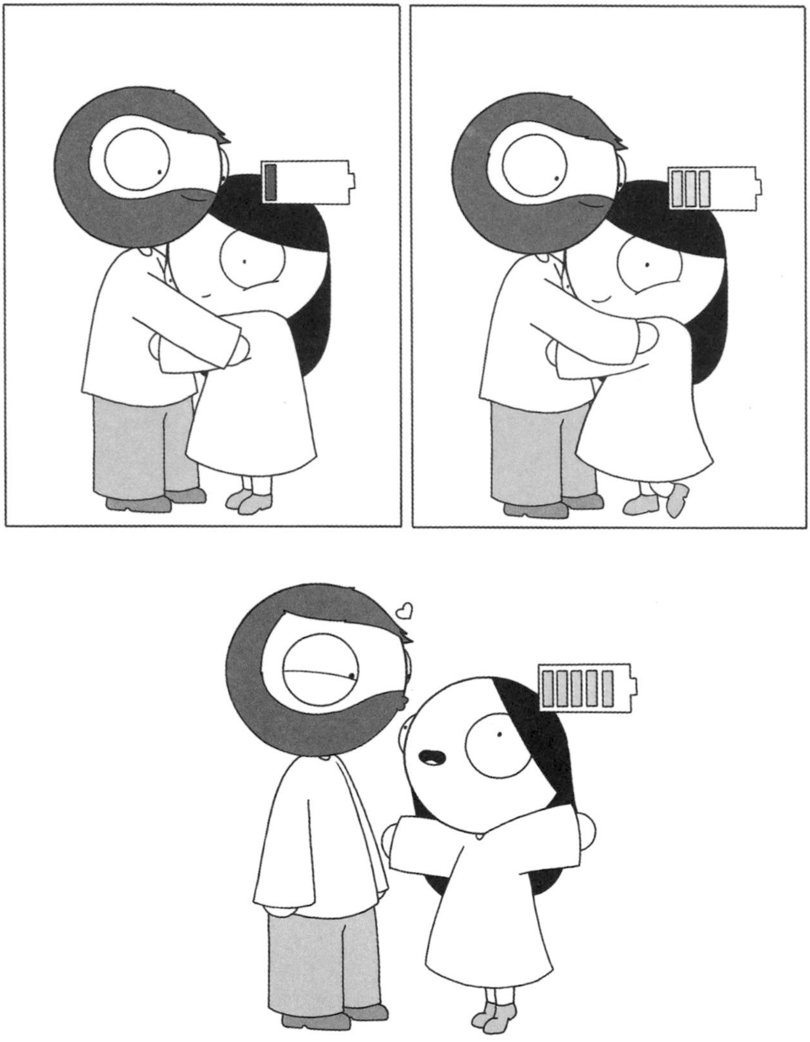

Taking Care of Your Drunk Girlfriend

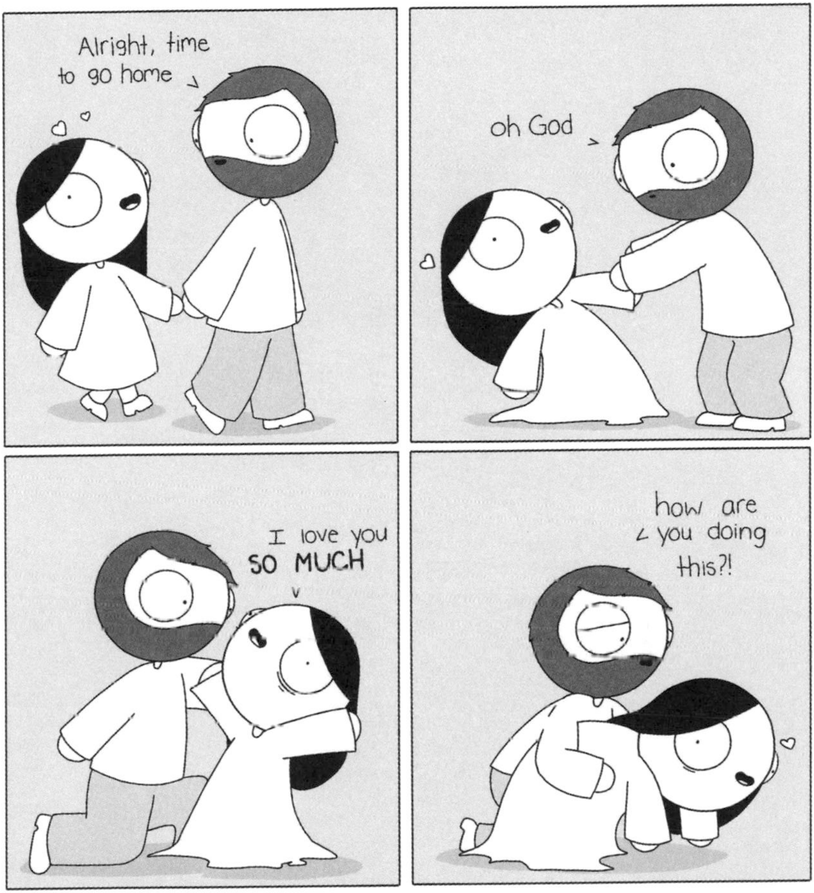

Alright, time to go home
oh God
I love you SO MUCH
how are you doing this?!

Pajamas Then

I'm just gonna put on some PJs
OK

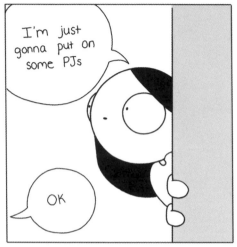

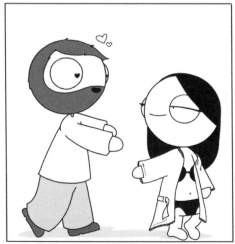

Pajamas Now

I'm just gonna put on that sweatshirt of yours that i've claimed as PJ's
OK

Go ahead,
open it

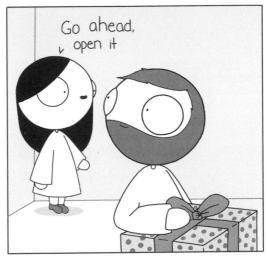

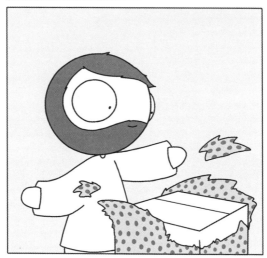

SURPRISE
It's a lifetime supply of my unconditional love!

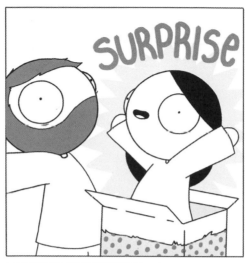

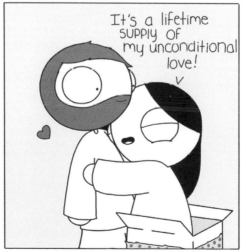

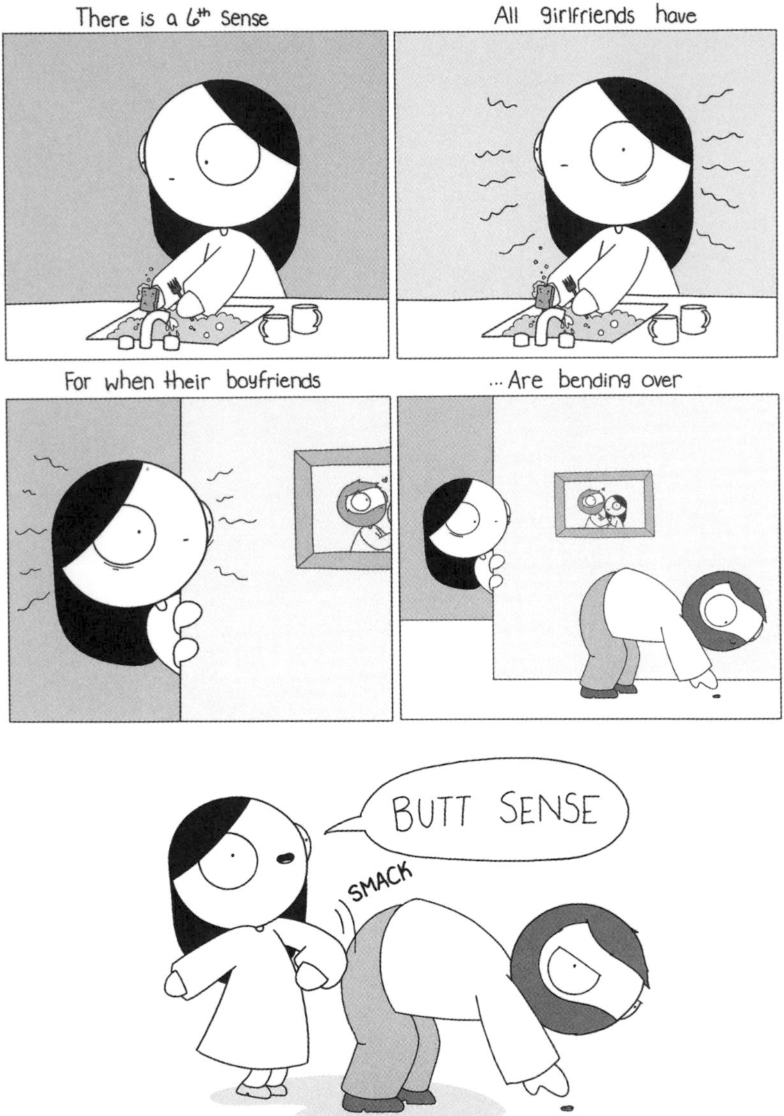
There is a 6th sense
All girlfriends have
For when their boyfriends
...Are bending over
BUTT SENSE
SMACK

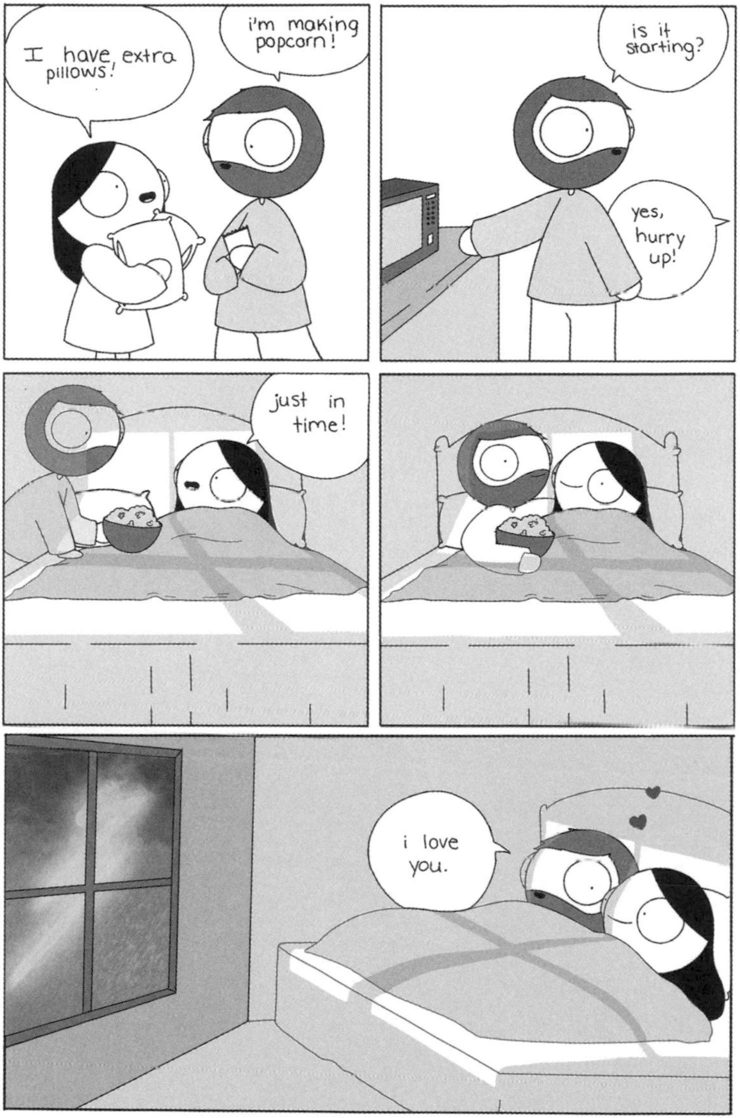
I have extra pillows!
i'm making popcorn!
is it starting?
yes, hurry up!
just in time!
i love you.

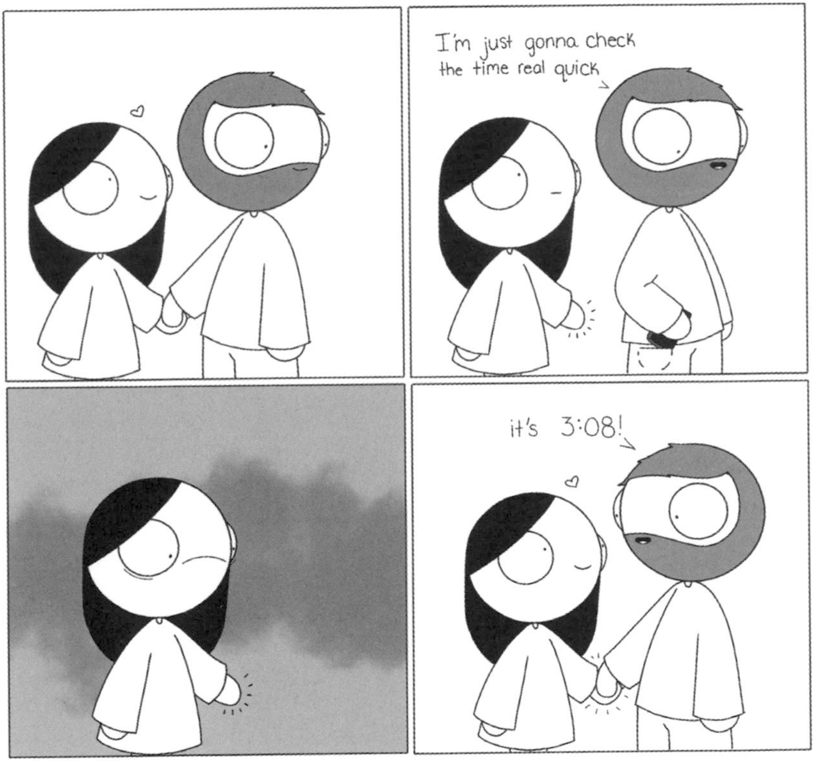
I'm just gonna check
the time real quick
it's 3:08!

When People come over after 10PM

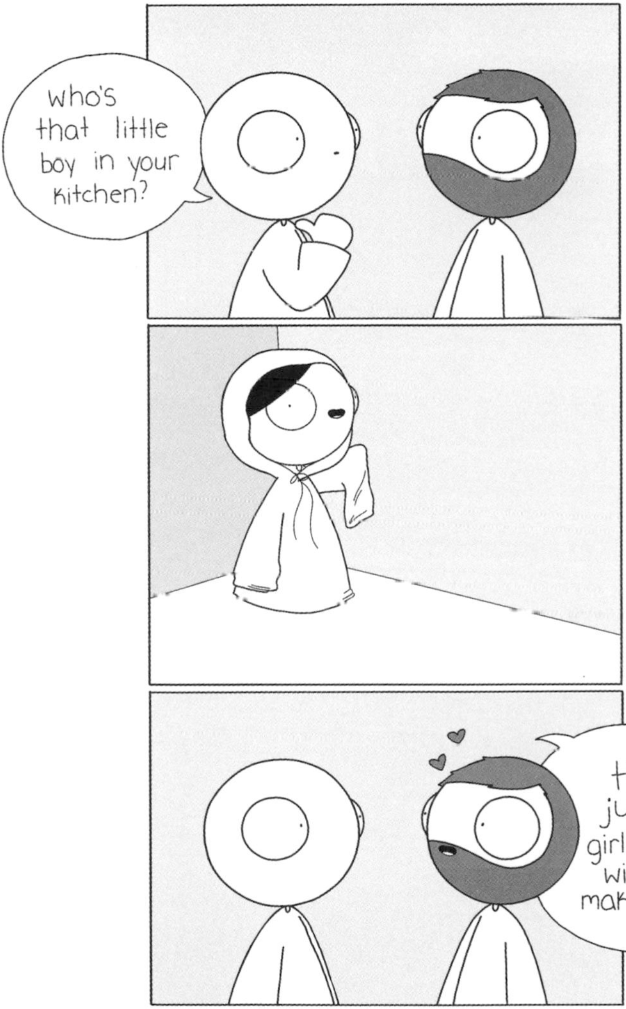
Who's that little boy in your kitchen?
that's just my girlfriend without makeup

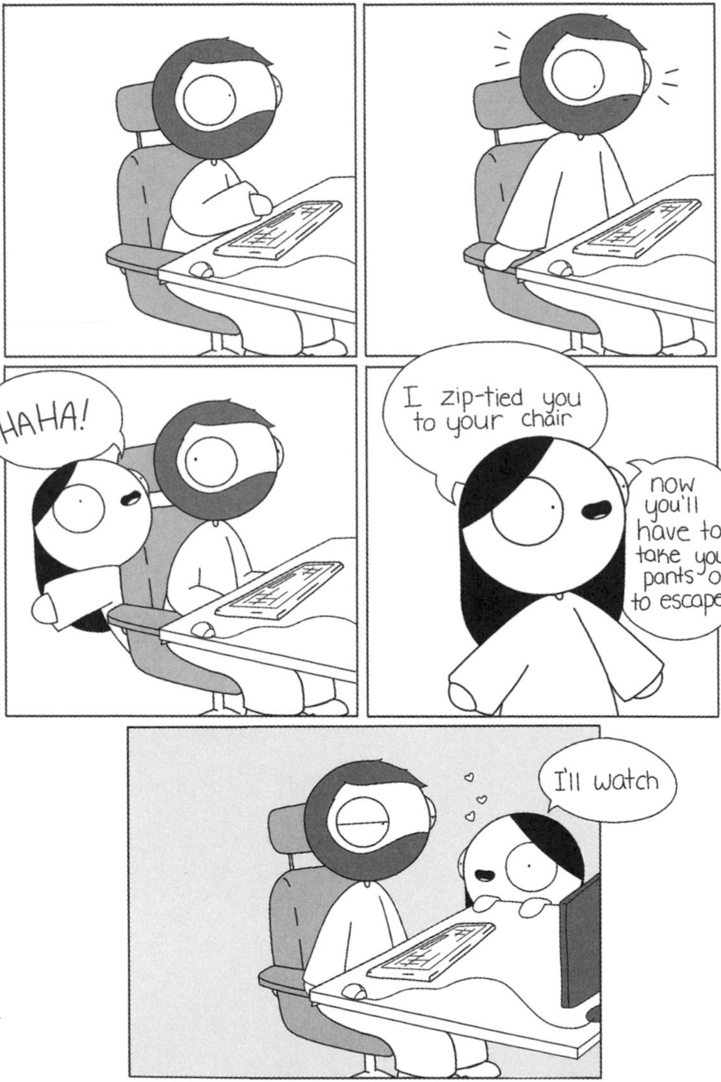
HAHA!
I zip-tied you to your chair
now you'll have to take your pants off to escape!
I'll watch

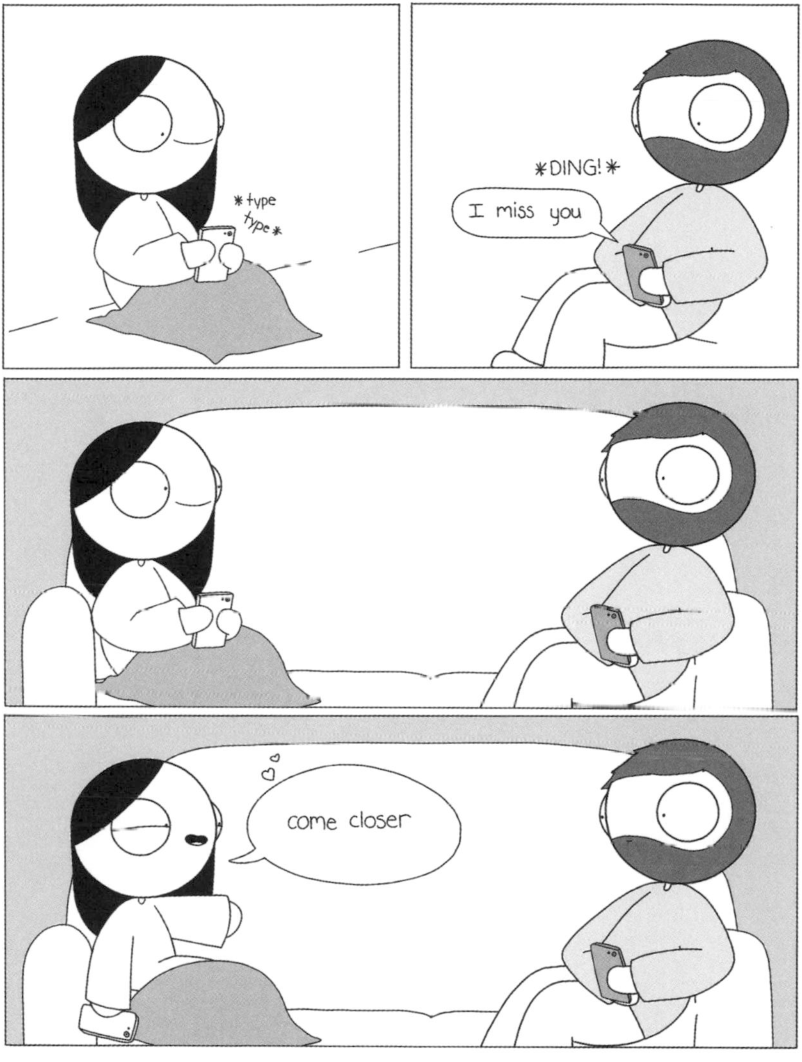
*type
type*
DING!
I miss you
come closer

"SUNDAYS"

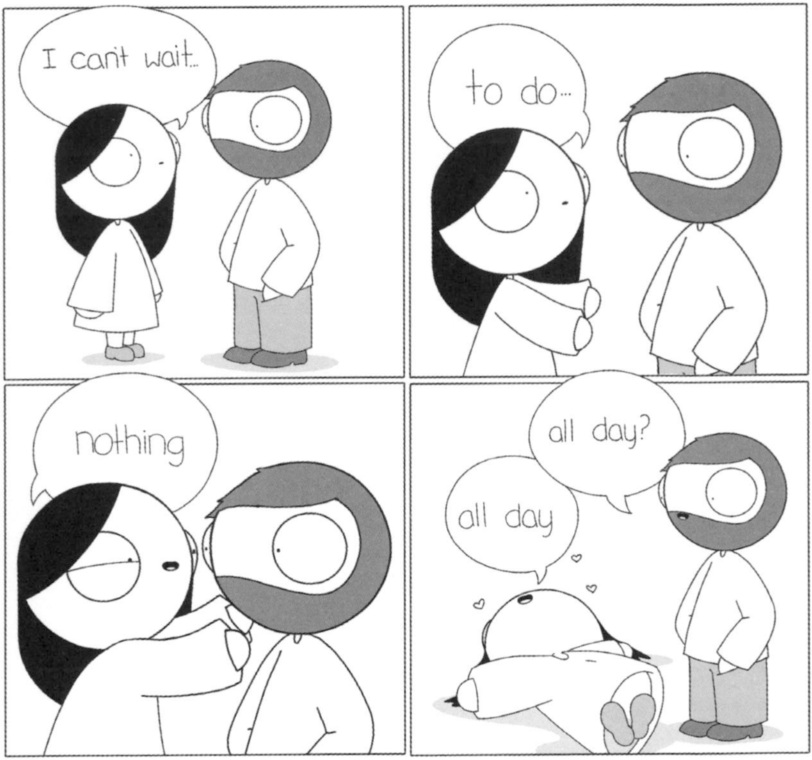
I can't wait...
to do...
nothing
all day?
all day

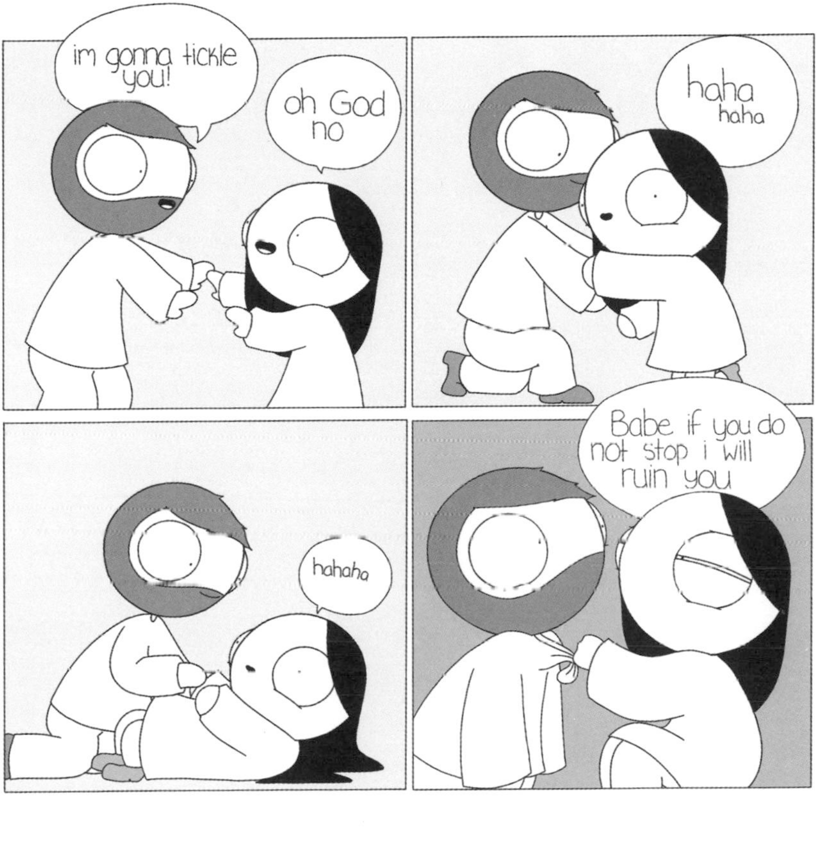
im gonna tickle you!
oh God no
haha haha
hahaha
Babe if you do not stop i will ruin you

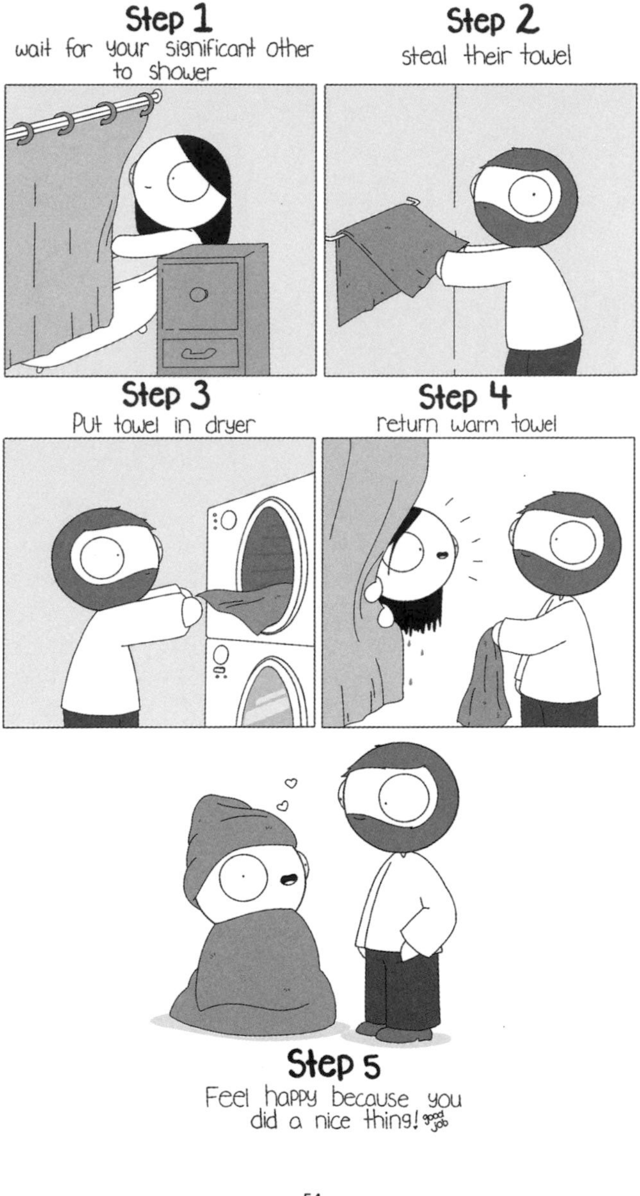
Step 1
wait for your significant other to shower
Step 2
steal their towel
Step 3
Put towel in dryer
Step 4
return warm towel
Step 5
Feel happy because you did a nice thing!
good job

"Height Difference"

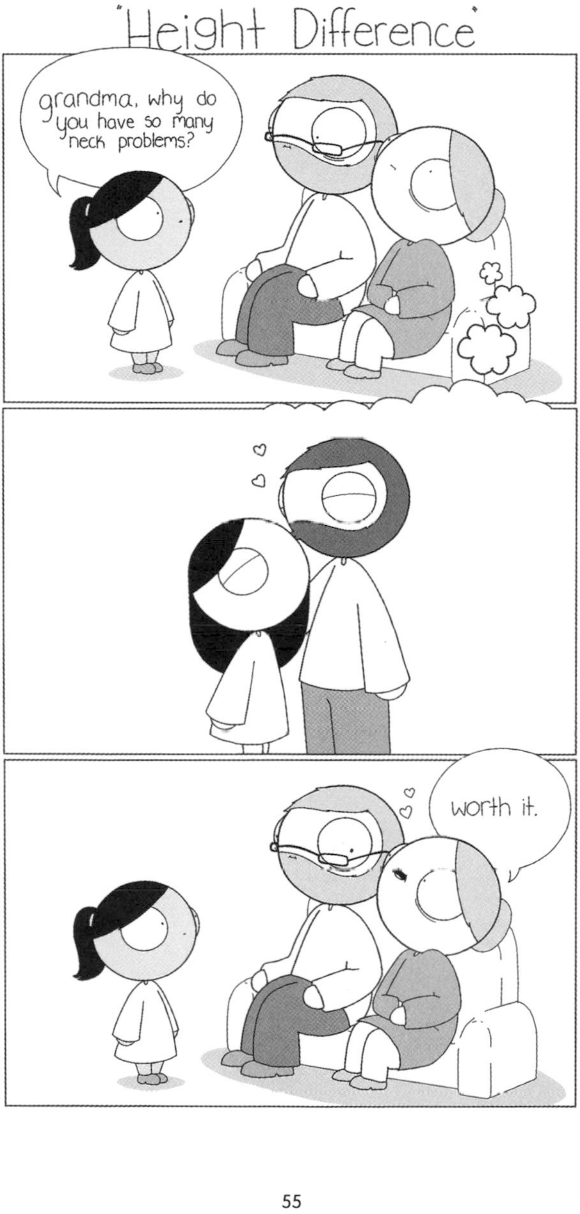
grandma, why do you have so many neck problems?
worth it.

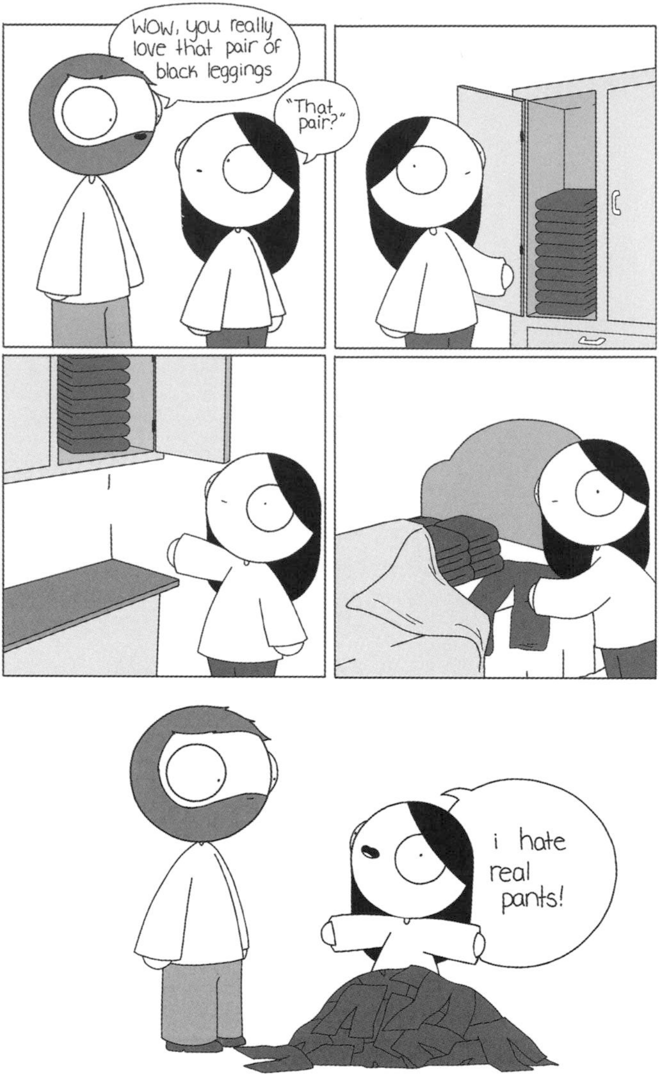
WOW, you really love that pair of black leggings
"That pair?"
i hate real pants!

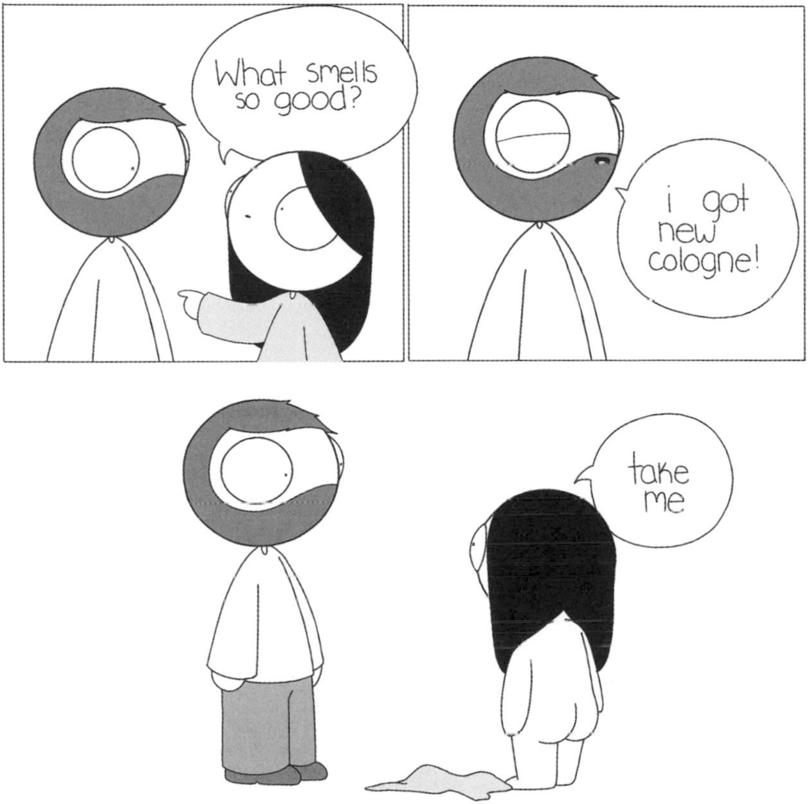
What smells so good?
i got new cologne!
take me

When he called me pretty back then
Really?
When he calls me pretty now
Still?

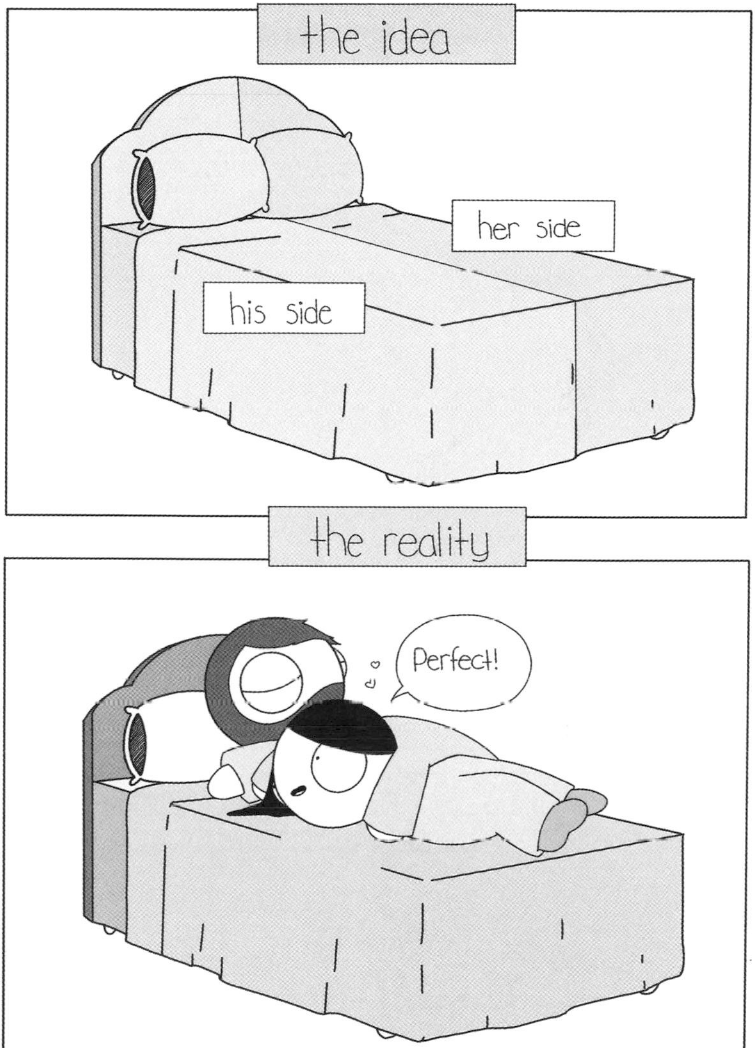
the idea
her side
his side
the reality
Perfect!

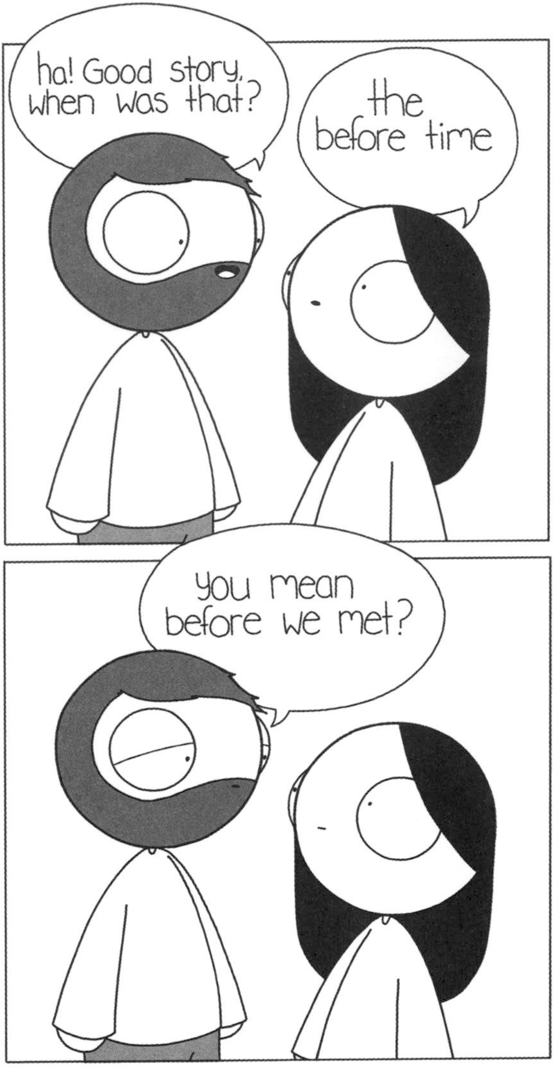
ha! Good story, when was that?
the before time
you mean before we met?

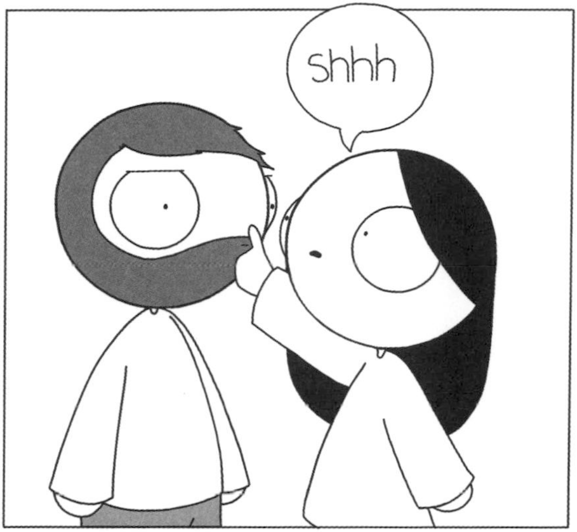
shhh

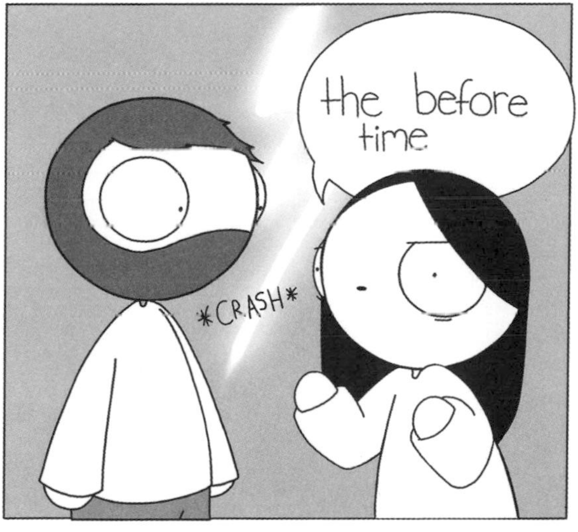
the before time
CRASH

Long-Term Relationship Flirting

i'm naked

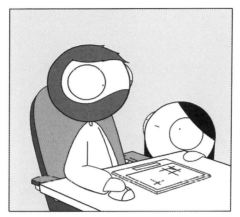

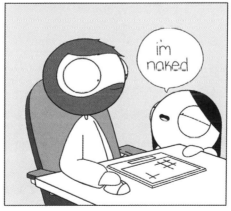

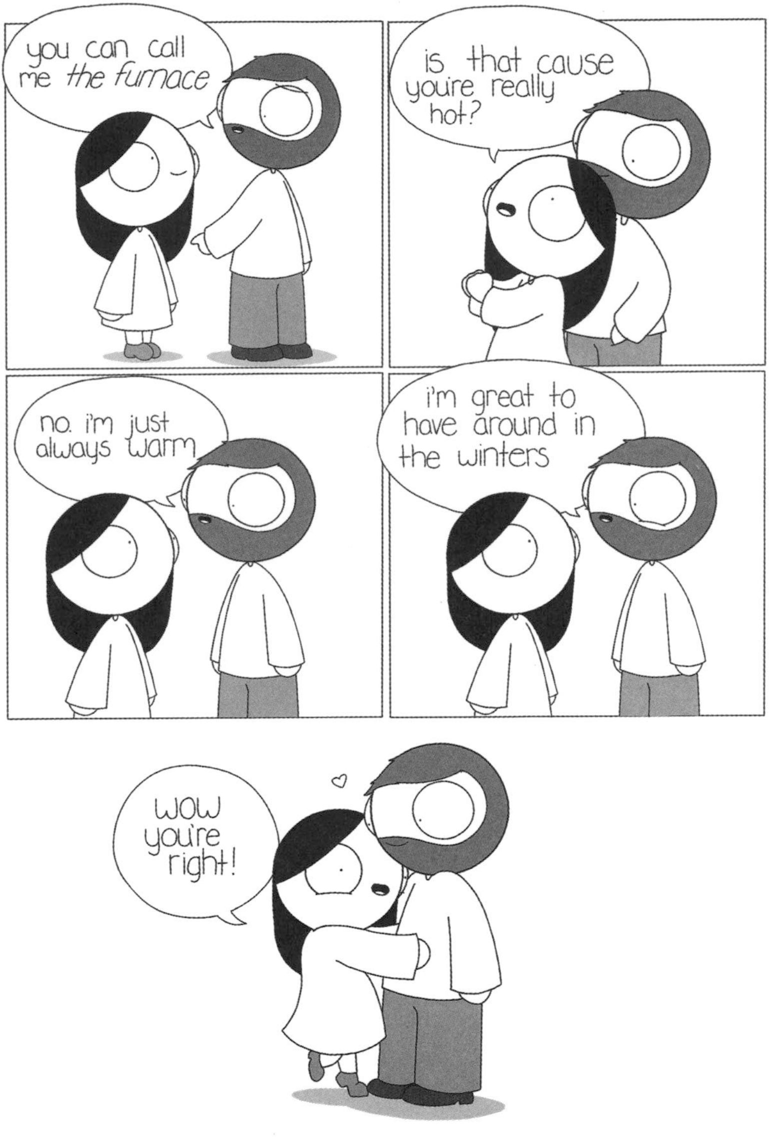
you can call me *the furnace*
is that cause you're really hot?
no. i'm just always warm
i'm great to have around in the winters
wow you're right!

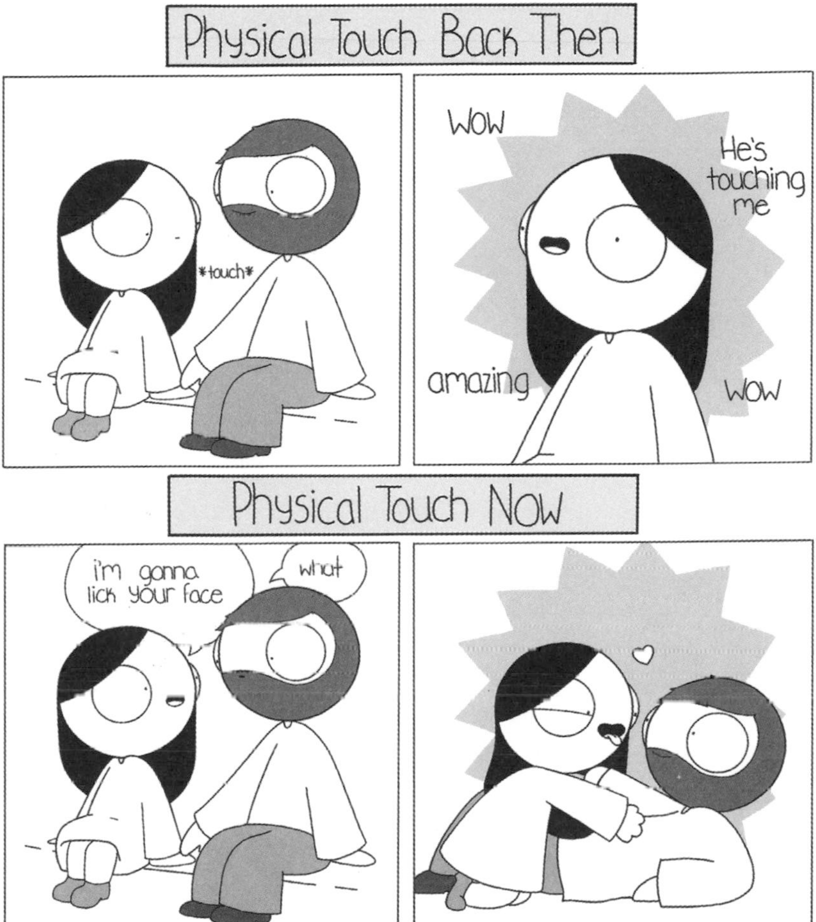

Physical Touch Back Then
touch
WOW
He's touching me
amazing
WOW
Physical Touch Now
i'm gonna lick your face
what

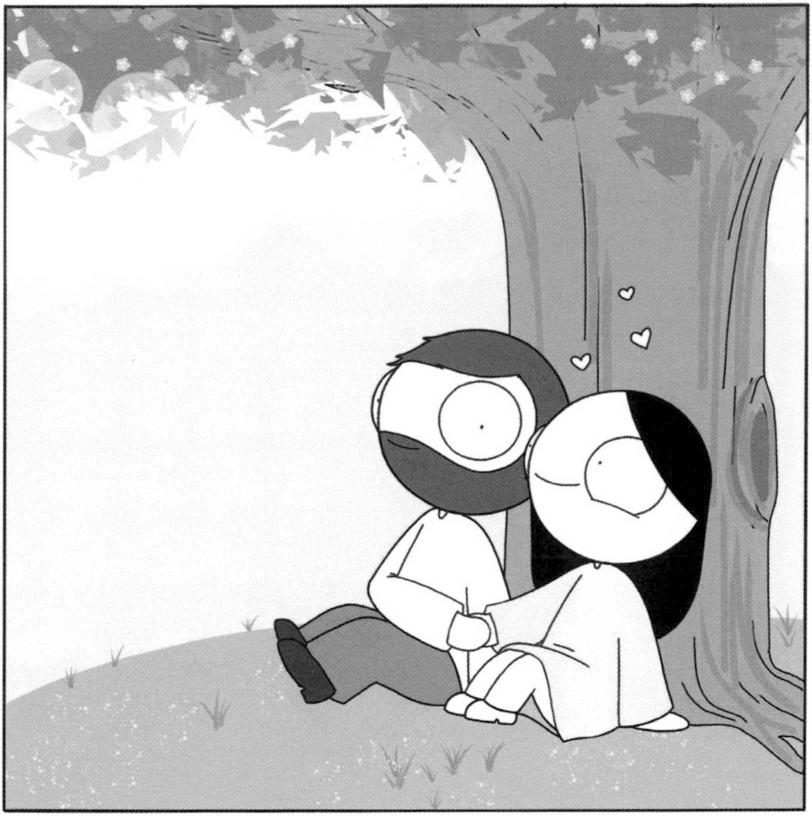

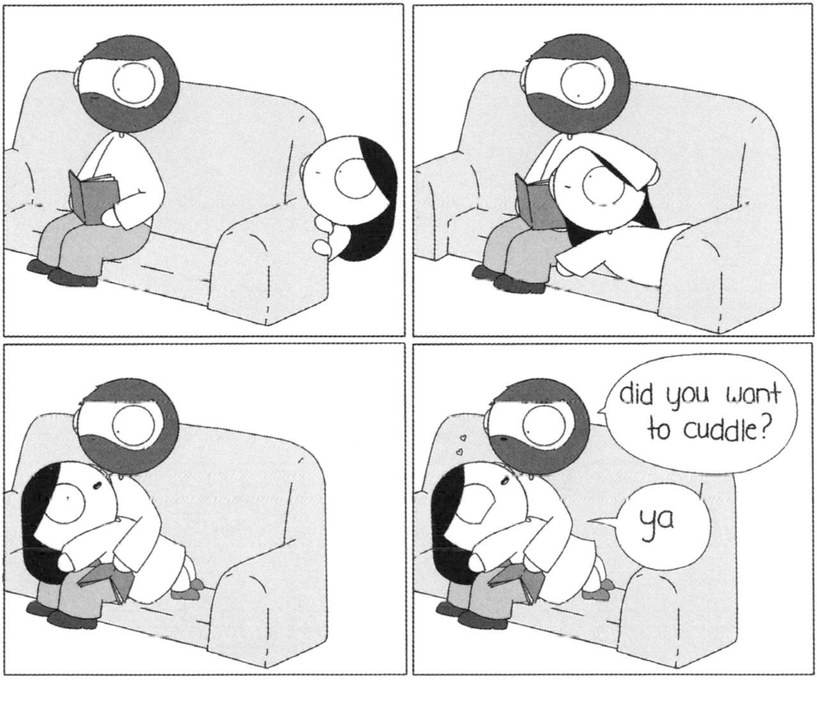
did you want to cuddle?
ya

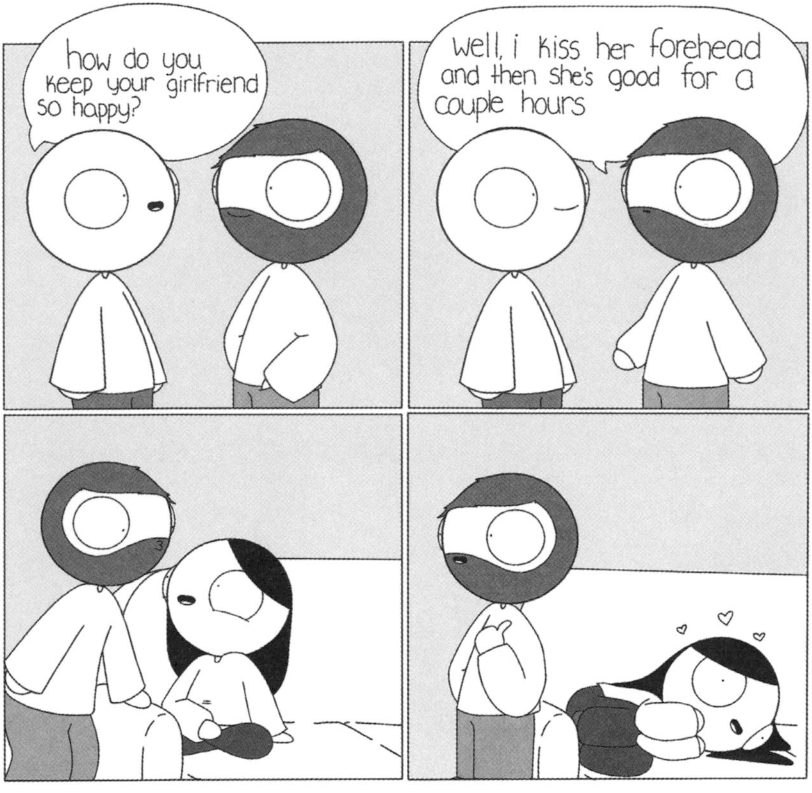
how do you keep your girlfriend so happy?
well, i kiss her forehead and then she's good for a couple hours

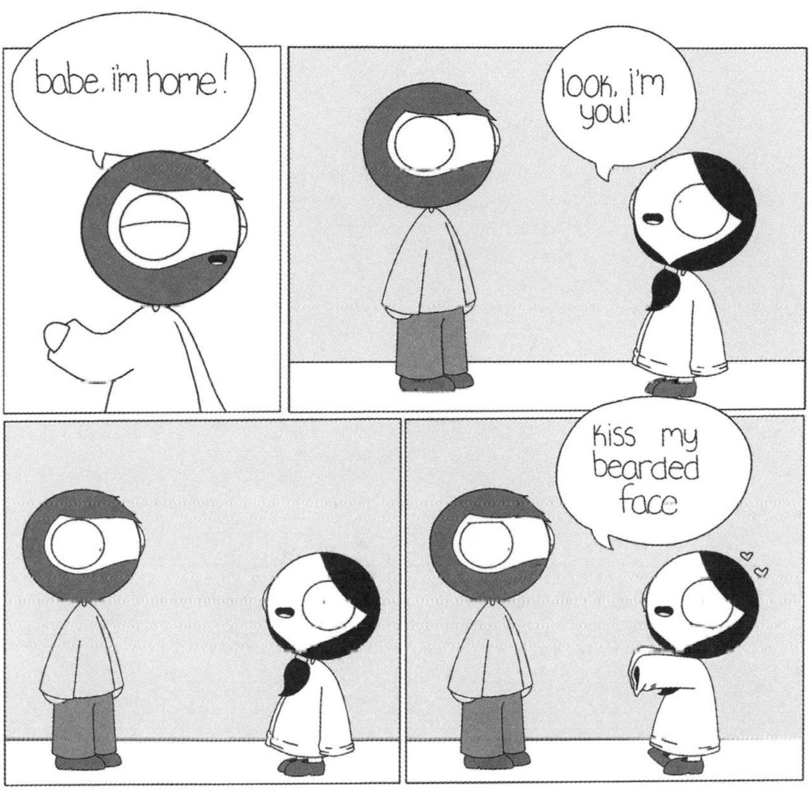
babe, i'm home!
look, i'm you!
kiss my bearded face

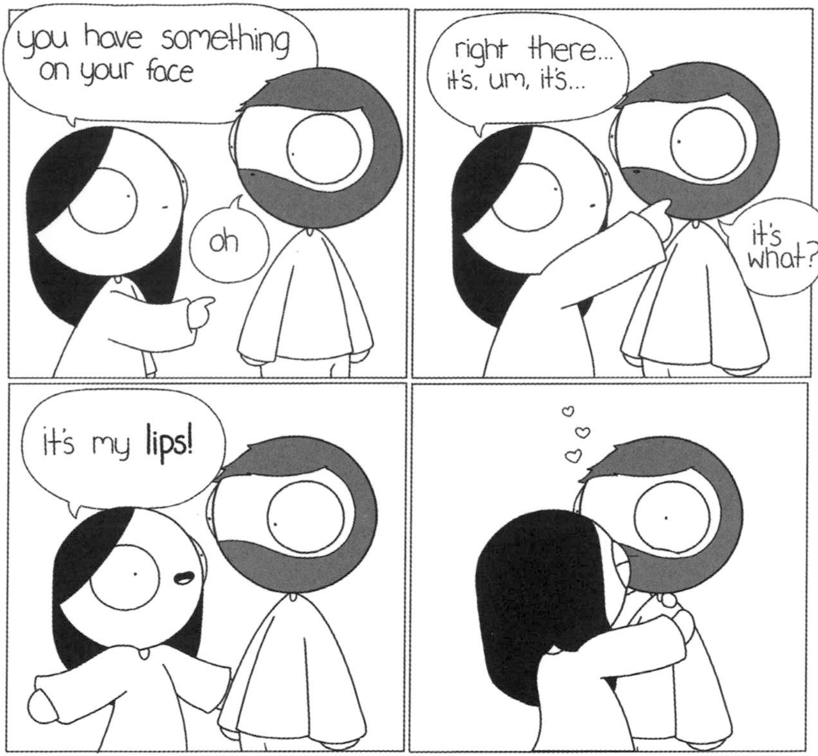
you have something on your face
oh
right there... it's, um, it's...
it's what?
it's my **lips!**

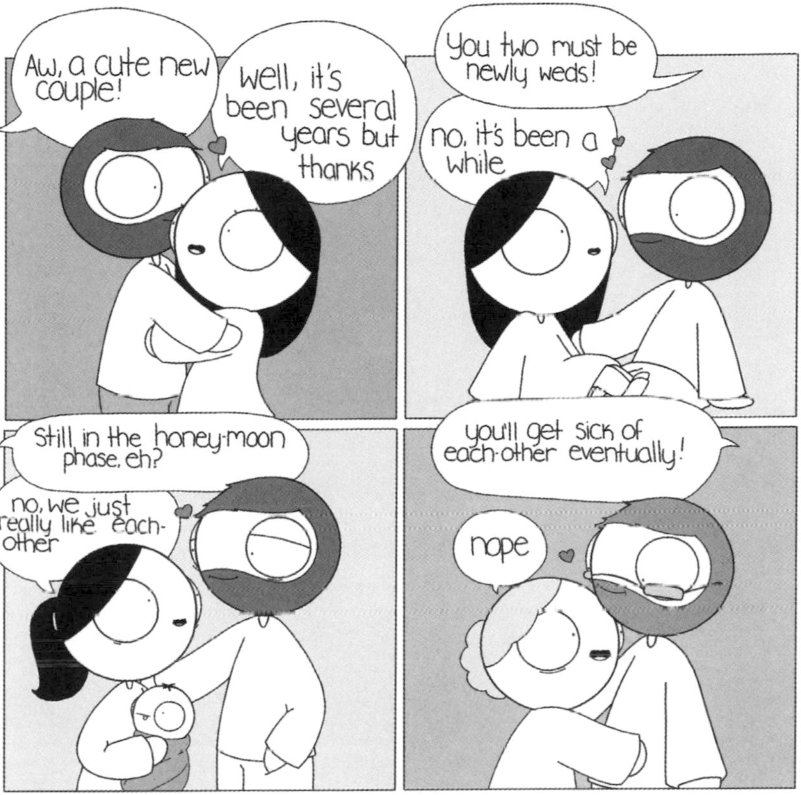
Aw, a cute new couple!
well, it's been several years but thanks
You two must be newly weds!
no, it's been a while
Still in the honey-moon phase, eh?
no, we just really like each-other
you'll get sick of each-other eventually!
nope

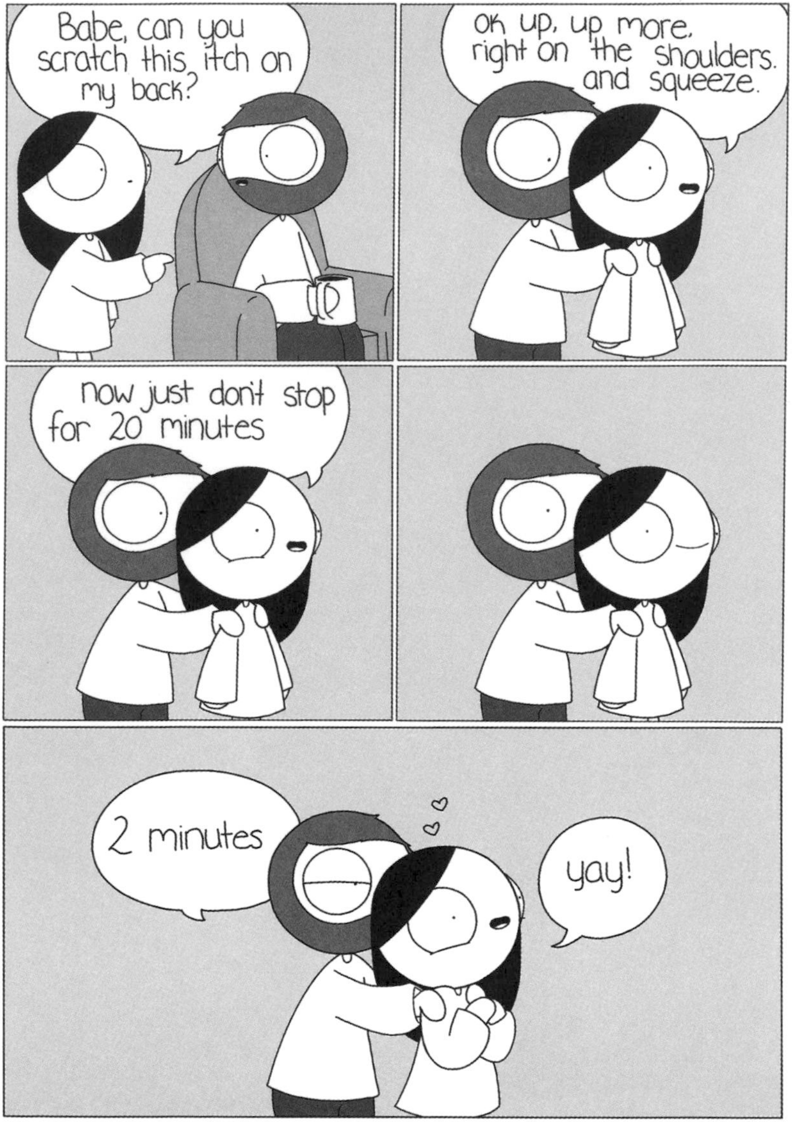
Babe, can you scratch this itch on my back?
ok up, up more. right on the shoulders. and squeeze.
now just don't stop for 20 minutes
2 minutes
yay!

DATE NIGHT : THEN

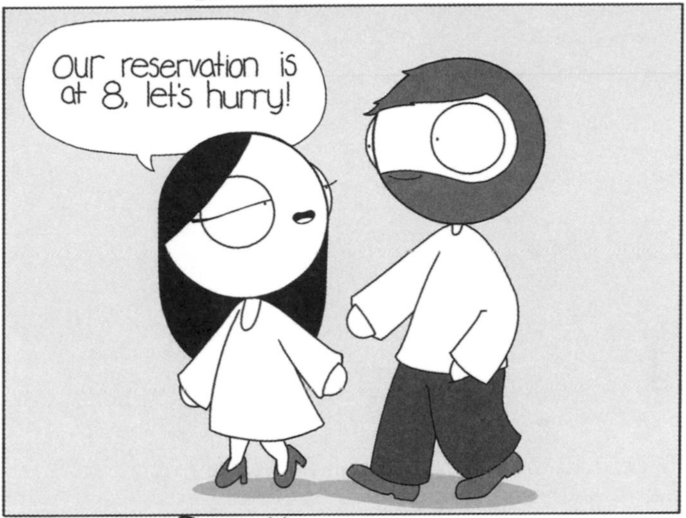
Our reservation is at 8, let's hurry!

DATE NIGHT : NOW

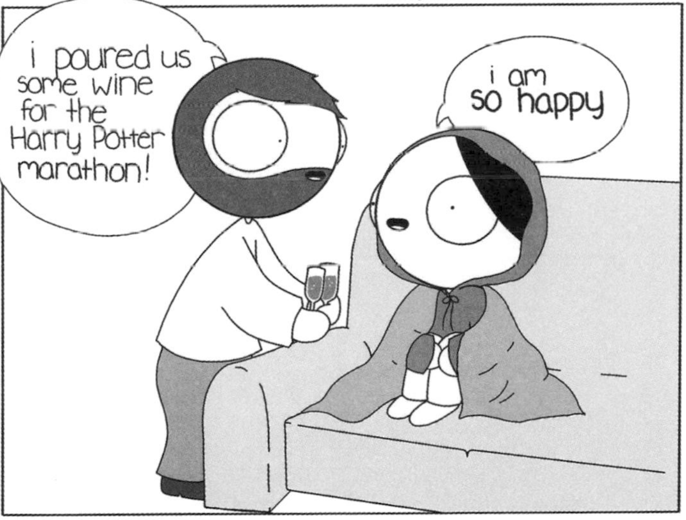
i poured us some wine for the Harry Potter marathon!
i am so happy

do i smell coffee..?
yes!
you woke up earlier than me and made me coffee?
yes!

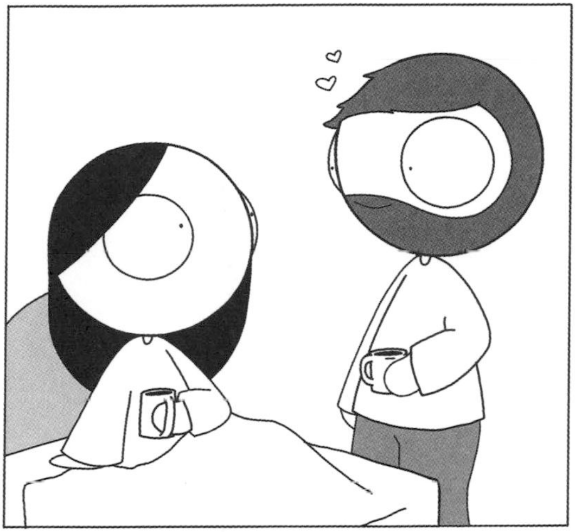

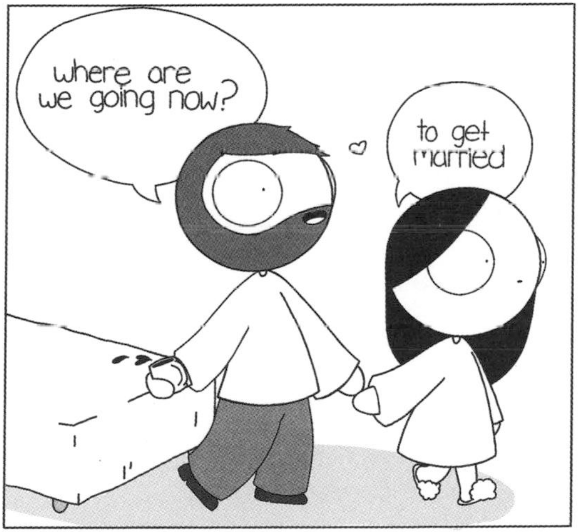
where are we going now?
to get married

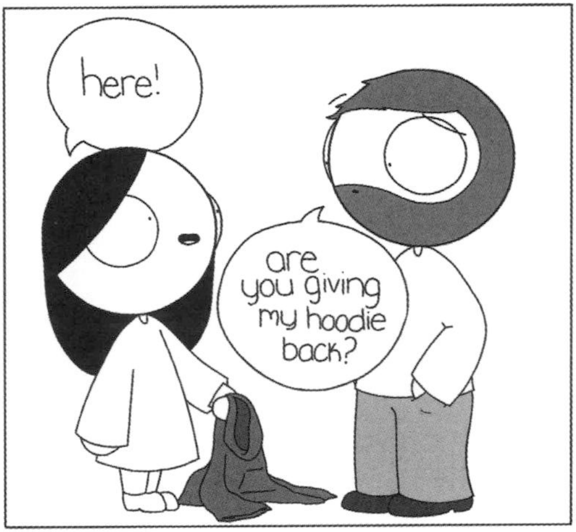
here!
are you giving my hoodie back?

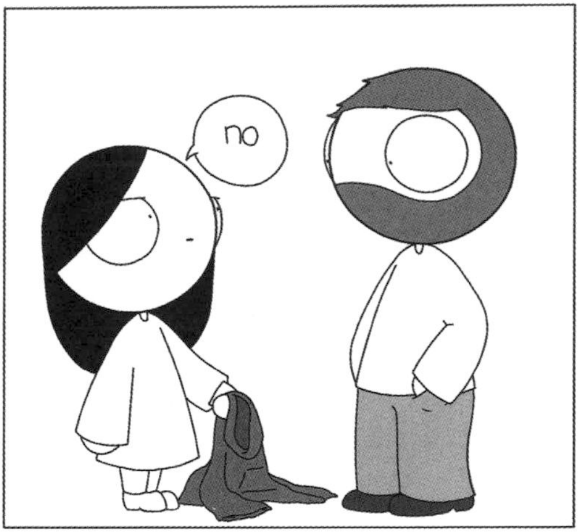
no

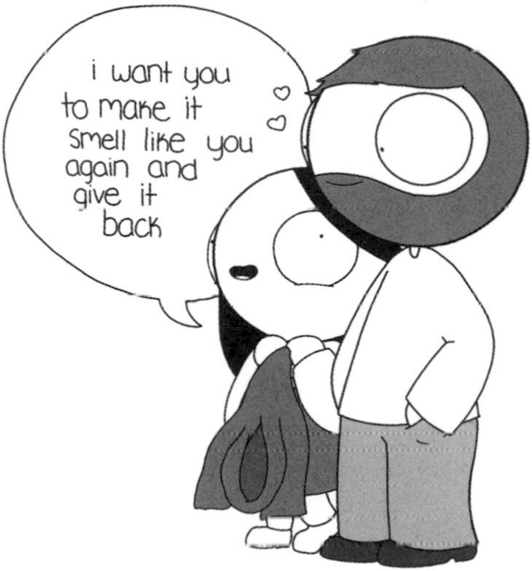
i want you to make it smell like you again and give it back

Texting: Socially Acceptable People

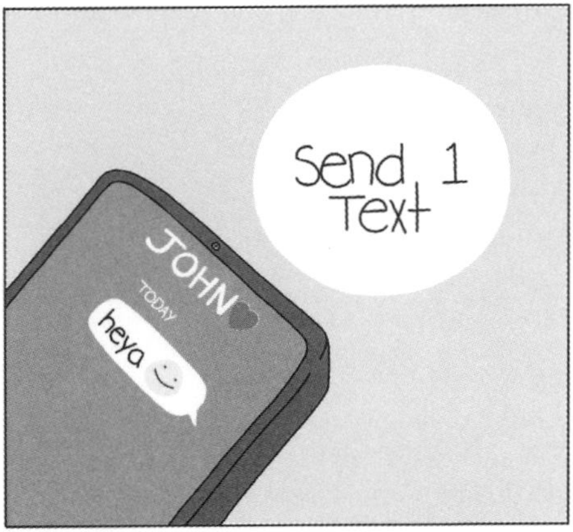
Send 1 Text
JOHN
TODAY
heya

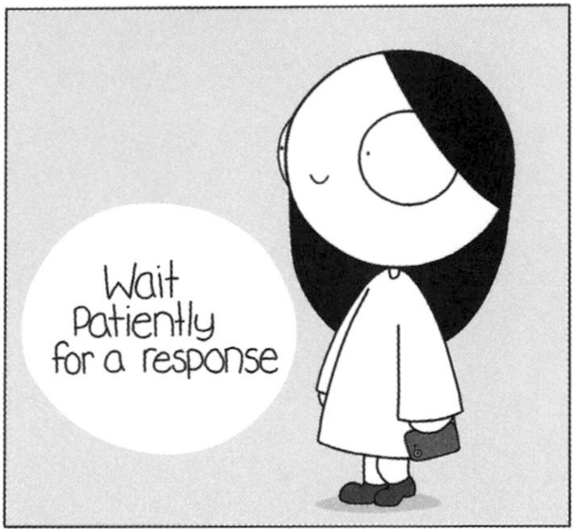
Wait Patiently for a response

Texting: Me

Send 1 Text
JOHN
TODAY
heya
Send 15 follow-up texts immediatley
babe, stop!
hiiiii
love me

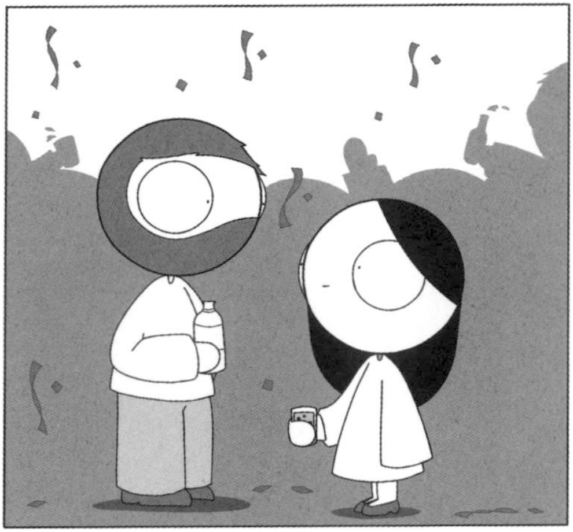

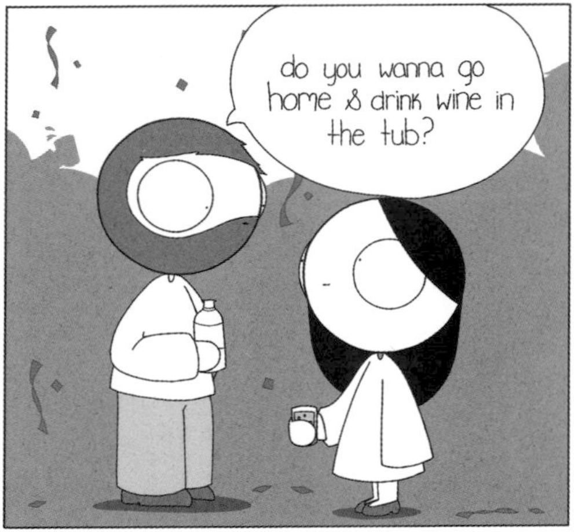
do you wanna go home & drink wine in the tub?

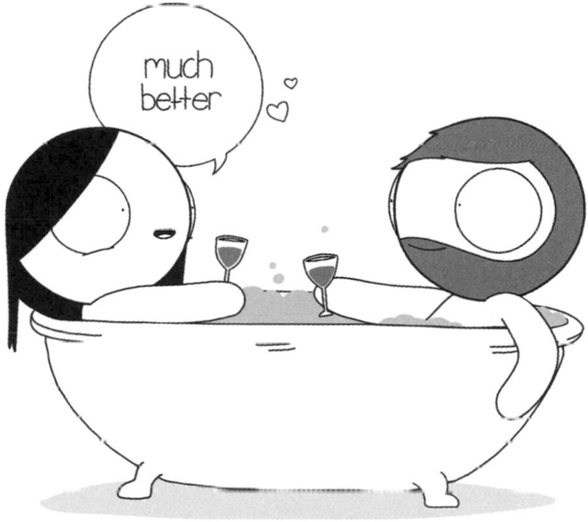
much better

When He Shows You off

LOOK

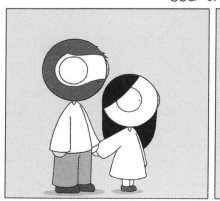

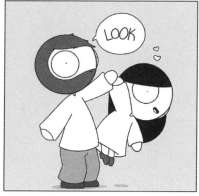

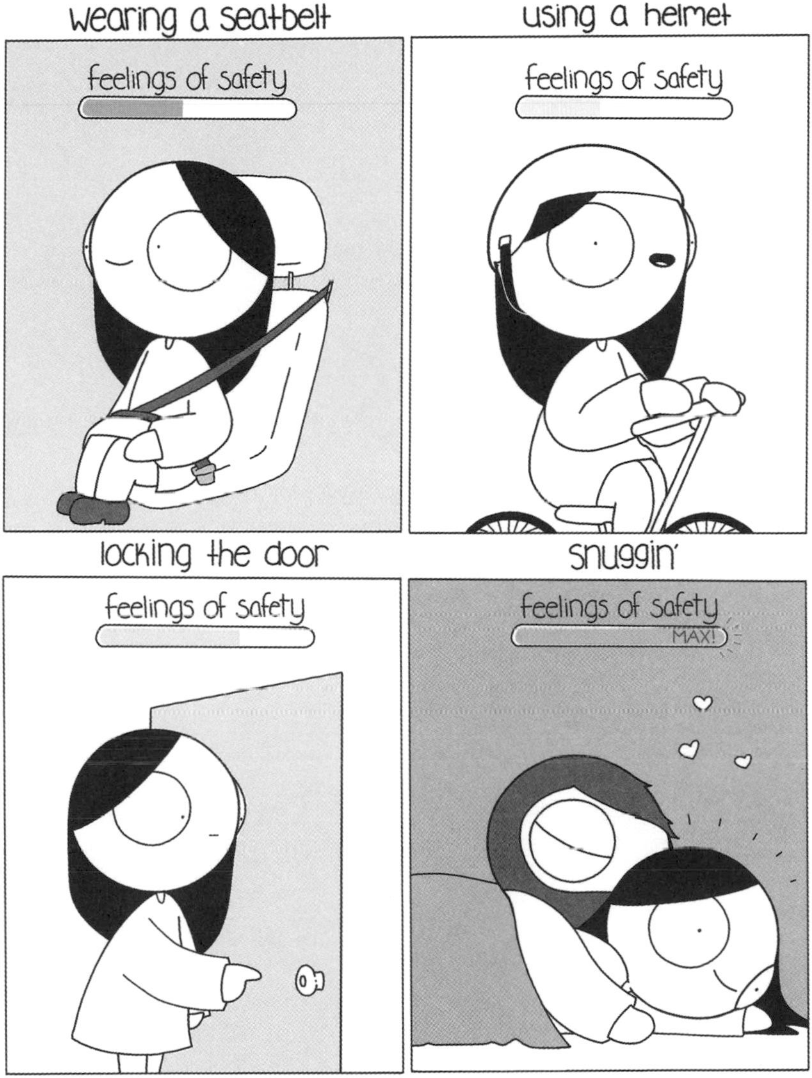
wearing a seatbelt
feelings of safety
using a helmet
feelings of safety
locking the door
feelings of safety
snuggin'
feelings of safety
MAX!

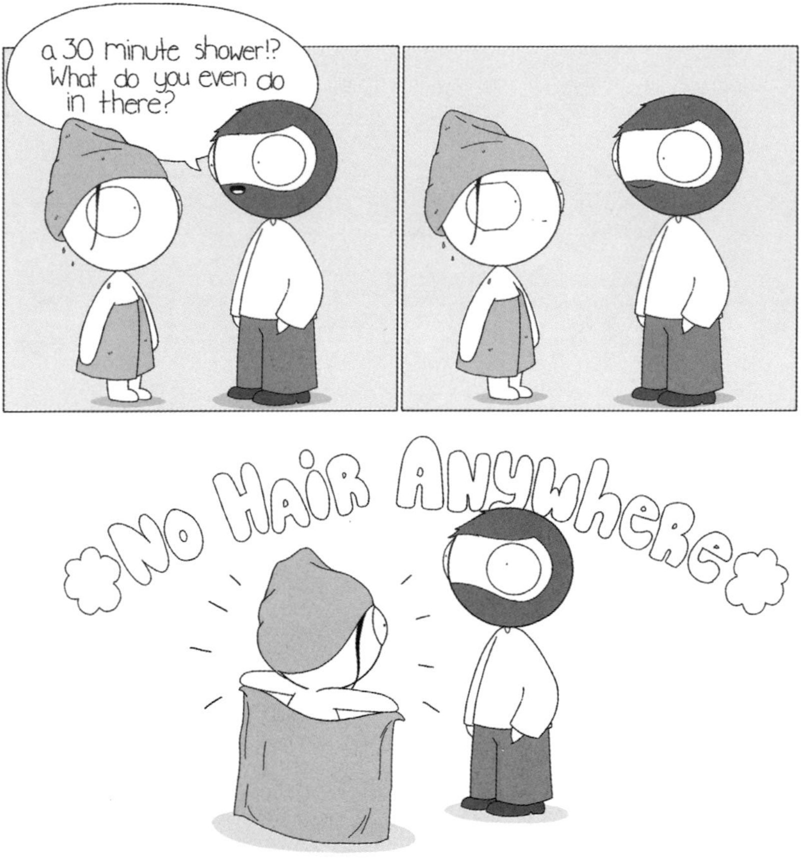
a 30 minute shower!? What do you even do in there?
No Hair Anywhere

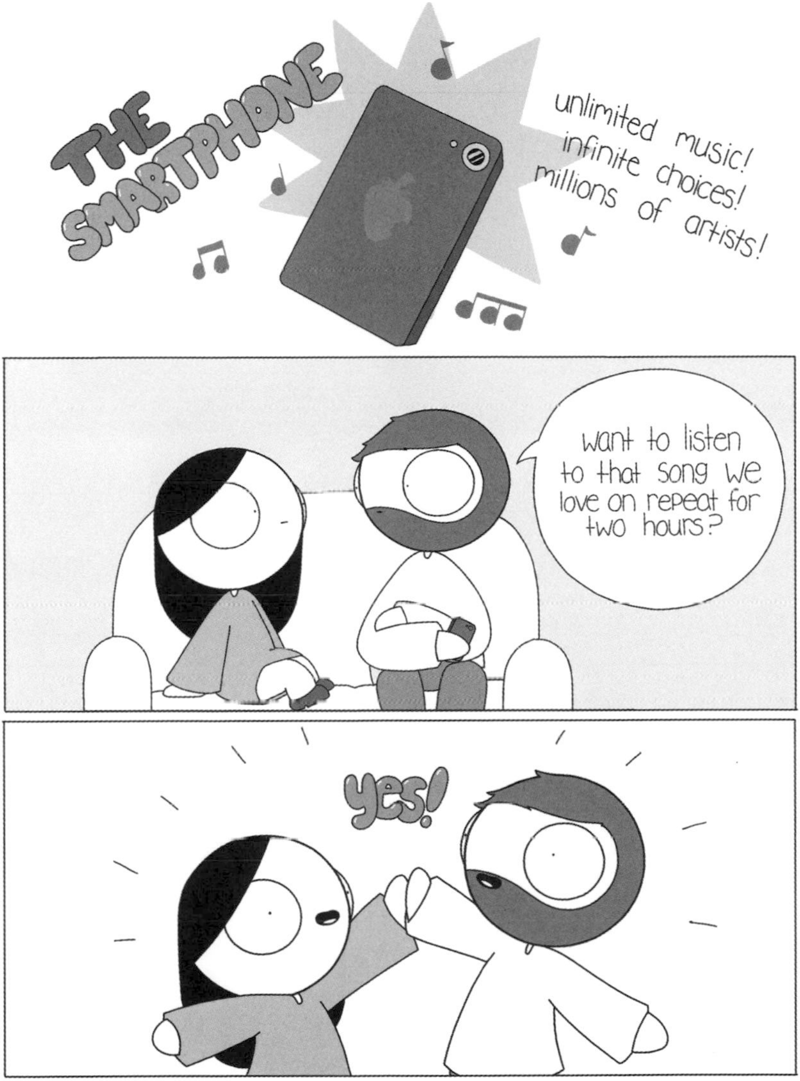
THE SMARTPHONE
unlimited music!
infinite choices!
millions of artists!
want to listen to that song we love on repeat for two hours?
YES!

What I Want

hey you
spontaneous kiss

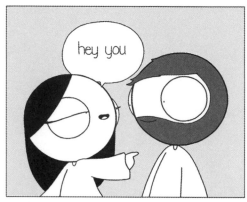

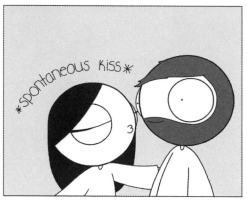

What Actually Happens

hey
can you lean down so i can spontaneously kiss you

Stressed Dog?

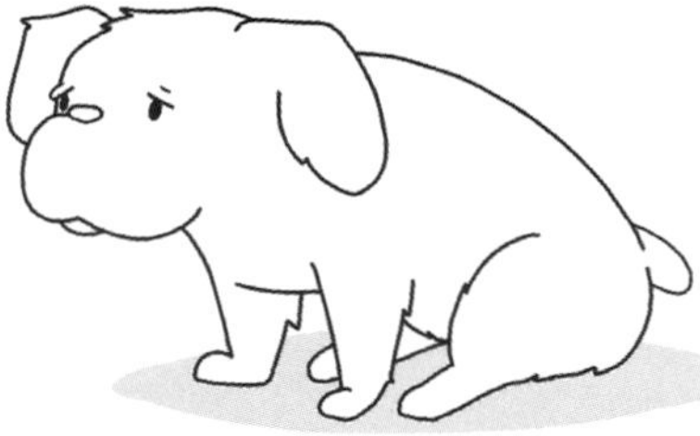

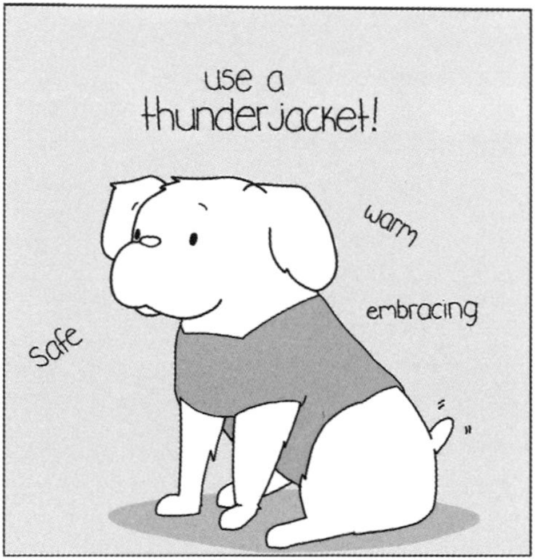
use a
thunderjacket!
warm
embracing
safe

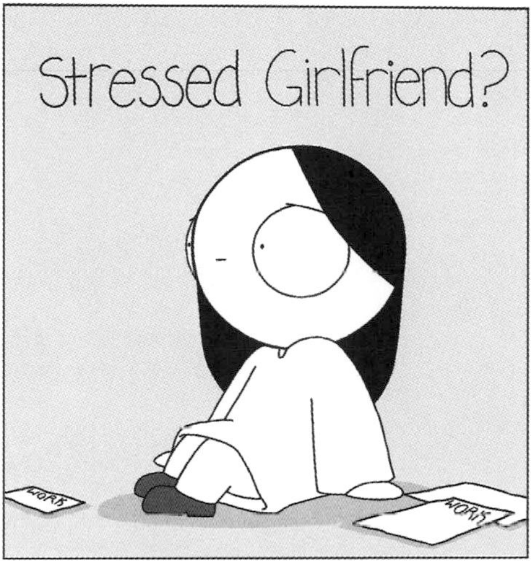
Stressed Girlfriend?
WORK
WORK

use a
thunderboyfriend!

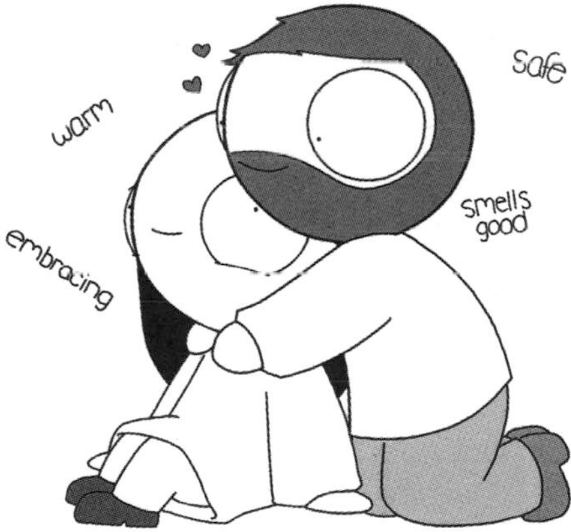
warm
safe
smells good
embracing

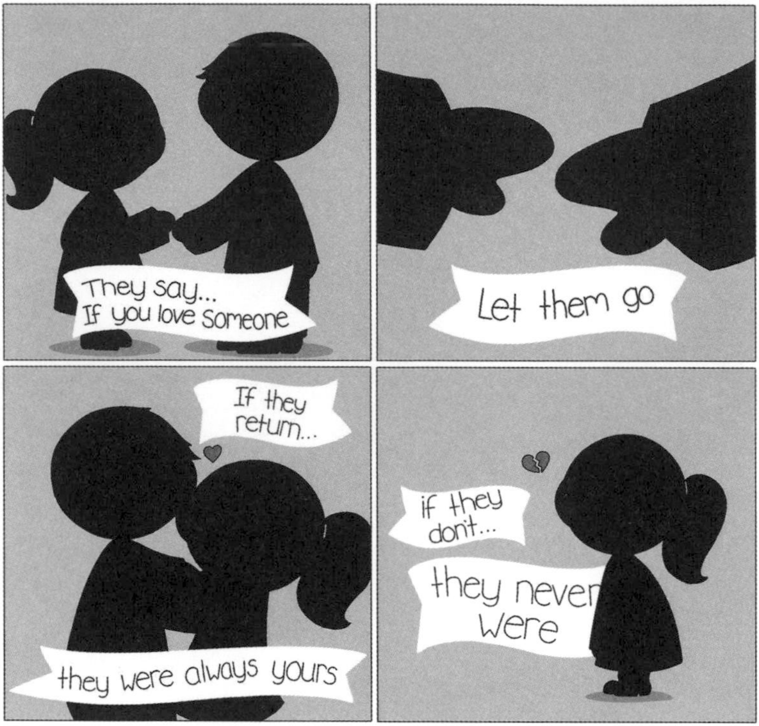
They say...
If you love someone
Let them go
If they return...
they were always yours
if they don't...
they never were

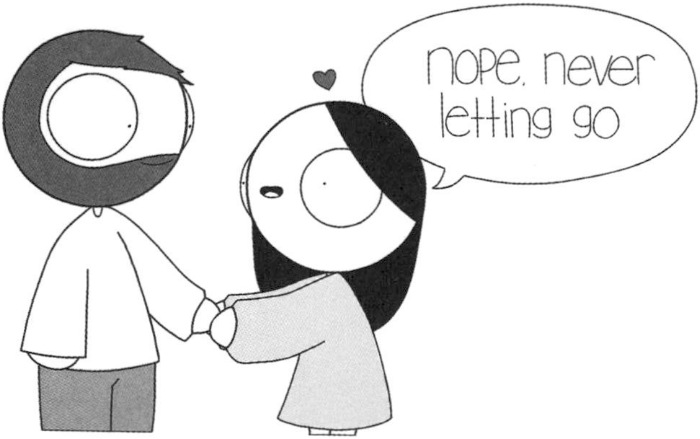
nope, never letting go

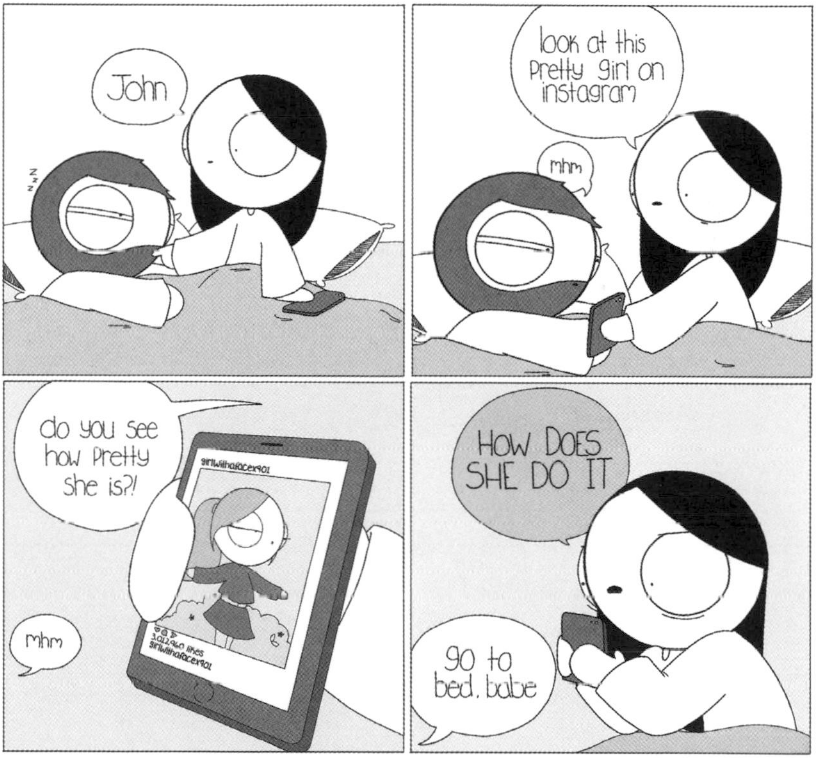
John
look at this pretty girl on instagram
mhm
do you see how pretty she is?!
girlwithafacex901
3,012,960 likes
girlwithafacex901
mhm
HOW DOES SHE DO IT
go to bed, babe

When A Guy in a Movie Does something Cute

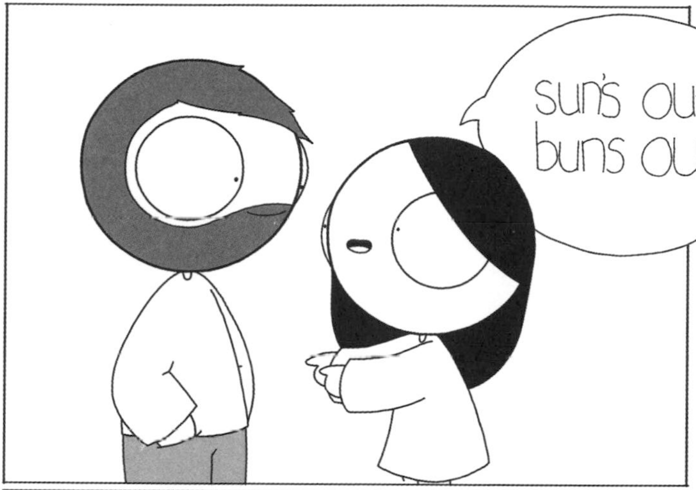
sun's out, buns out

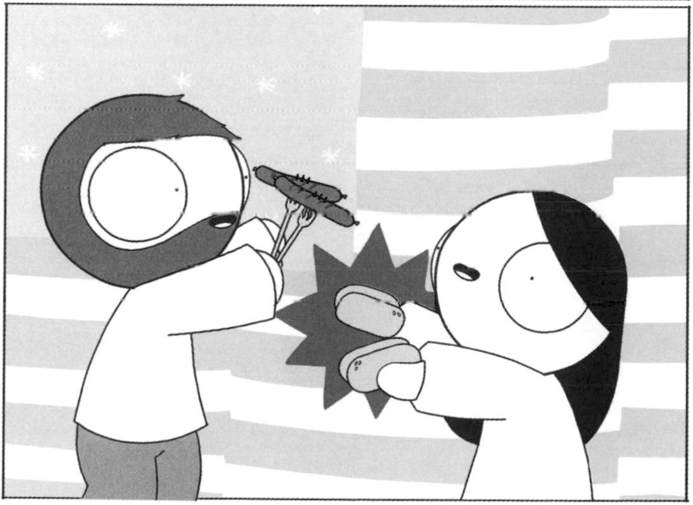

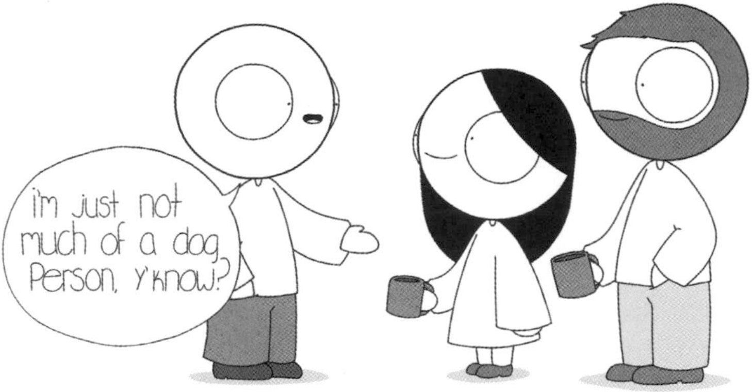
i'm just not much of a dog Person, y'know?

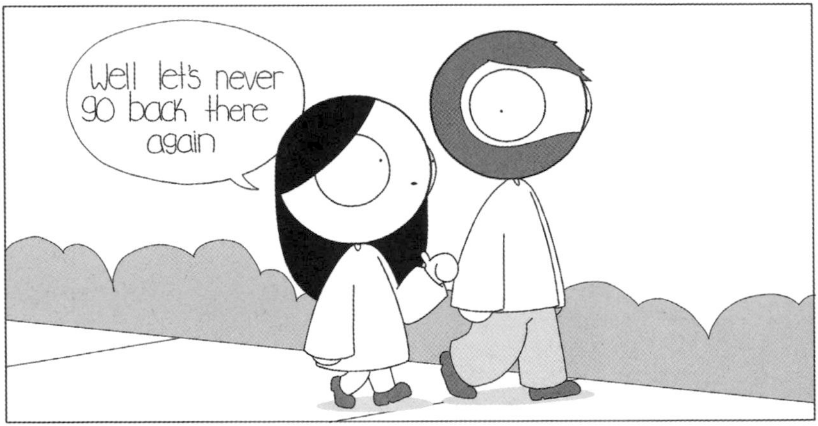
Well let's never go back there again

How To Pause Your Girlfriend

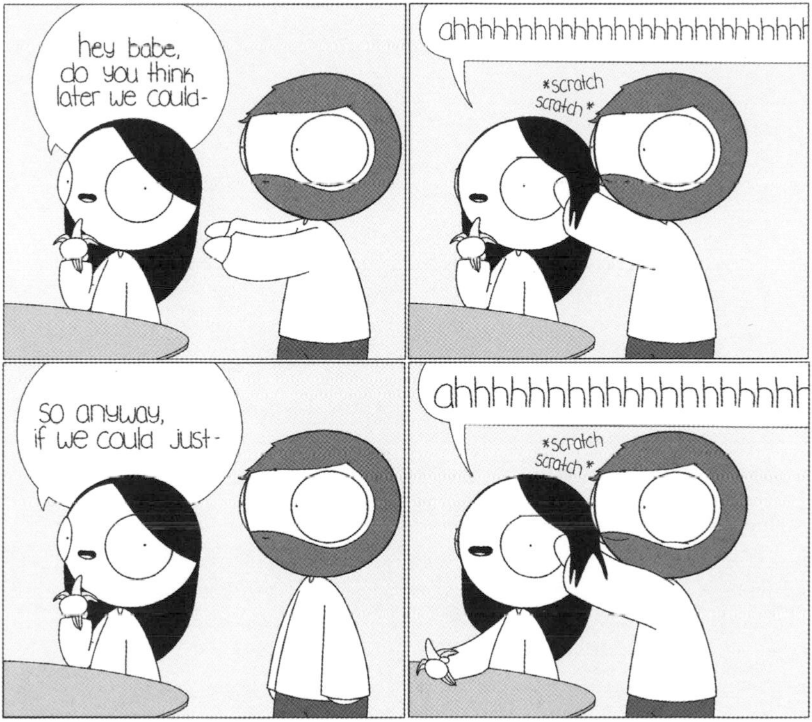
hey babe, do you think later we could-
ahhhhhhhhhhhhhhhhhhhhhhhhhhh
scratch scratch
so anyway, if we could just-
ahhhhhhhhhhhhhhhhh
scratch scratch

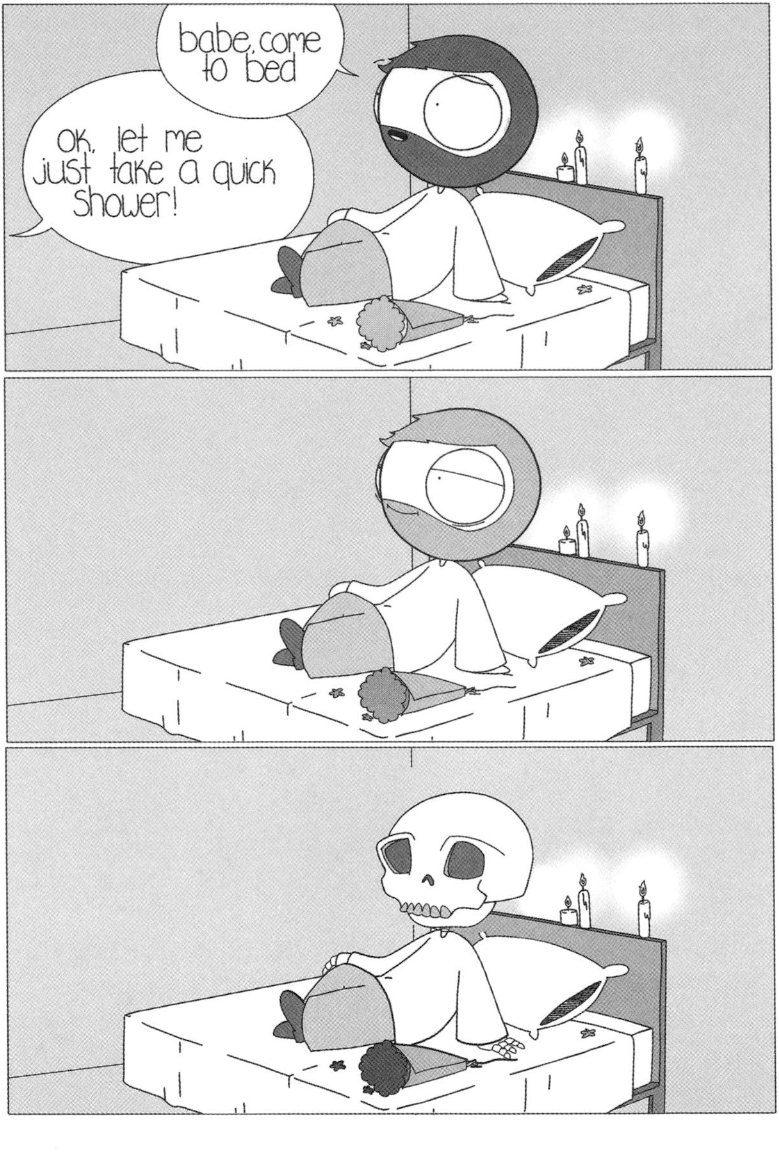
babe, come to bed
OK, let me just take a quick shower!

Cuddling In Summer

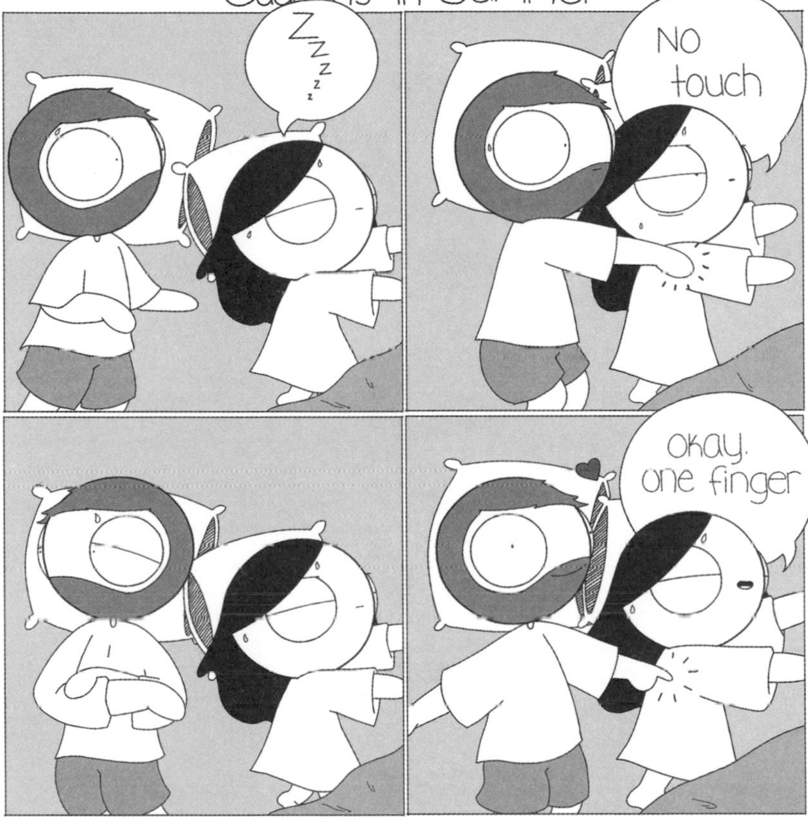
Z Z Z z z z
No touch
okay. one finger

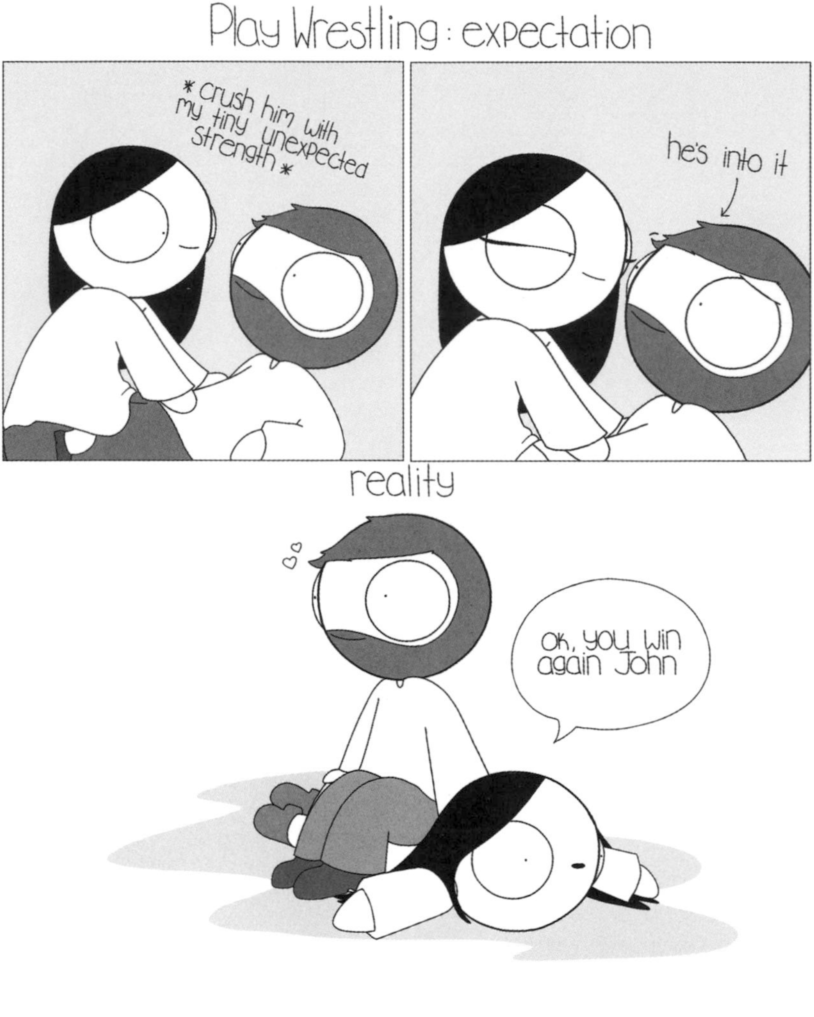
Play Wrestling : expectation
crush him with my tiny unexpected strength
he's into it
reality
ok, you win again John

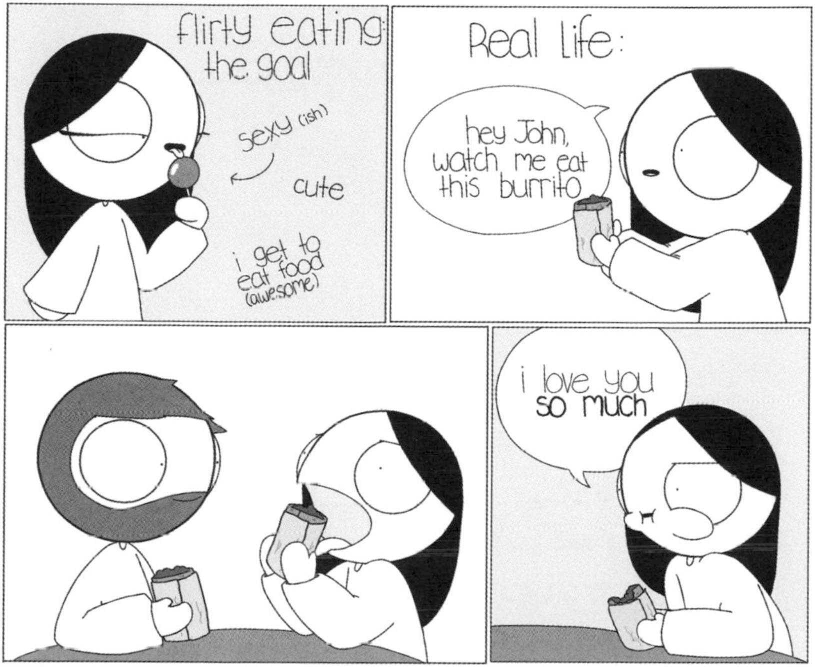
flirty eating:
the goal
sexy (ish)
cute
i get to
eat food
(awesome)
Real Life:
hey John,
watch me eat
this burrito
i love you
so much

What I'm Worried He'll Notice

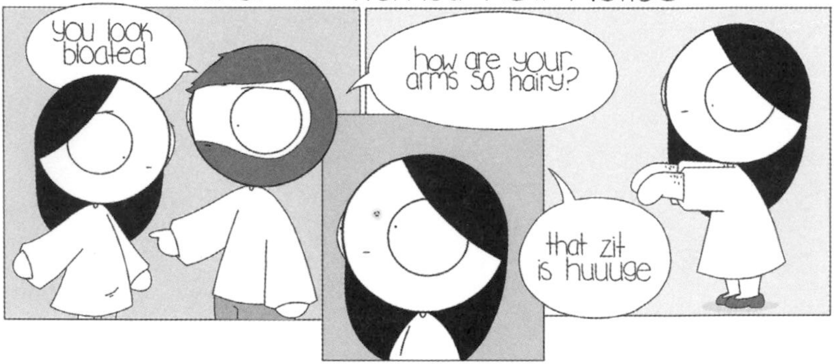
you look bloated
how are your arms so hairy?
that zit is huuuge

What He Actually Notices

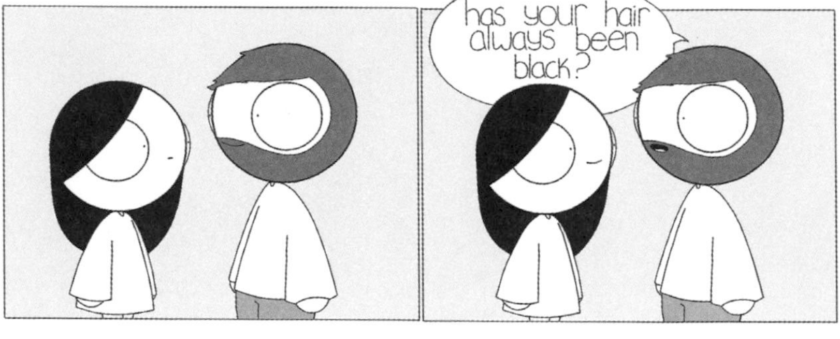
has your hair always been black?

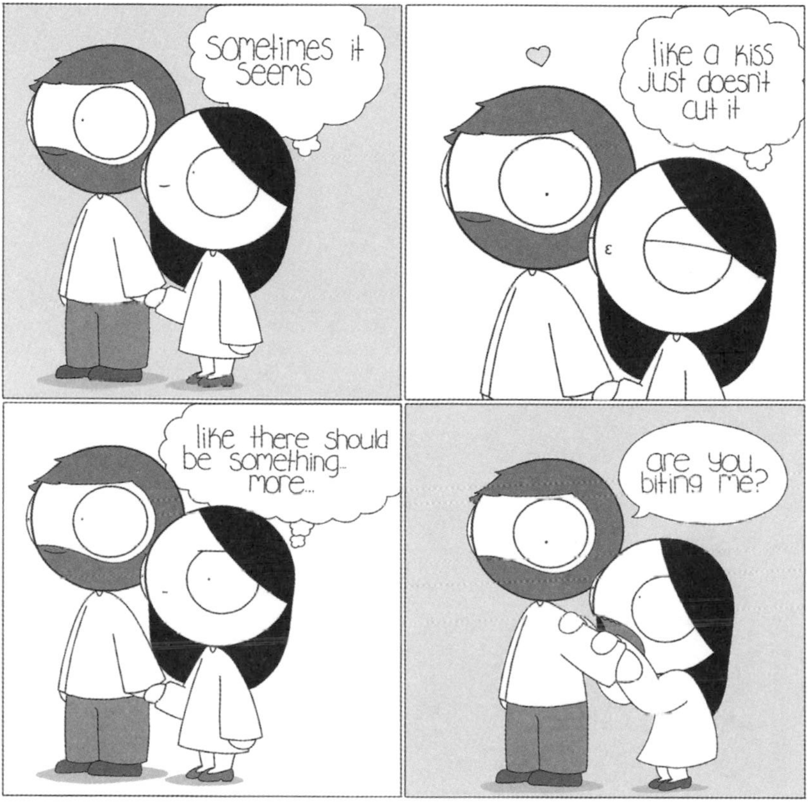
Sometimes it seems
like a kiss just doesn't cut it
like there should be something... more...
are you biting me?

when i hold the umbrella
when he holds the umbrella
solution: stay inside & watch movies instead
i love rainy days with you

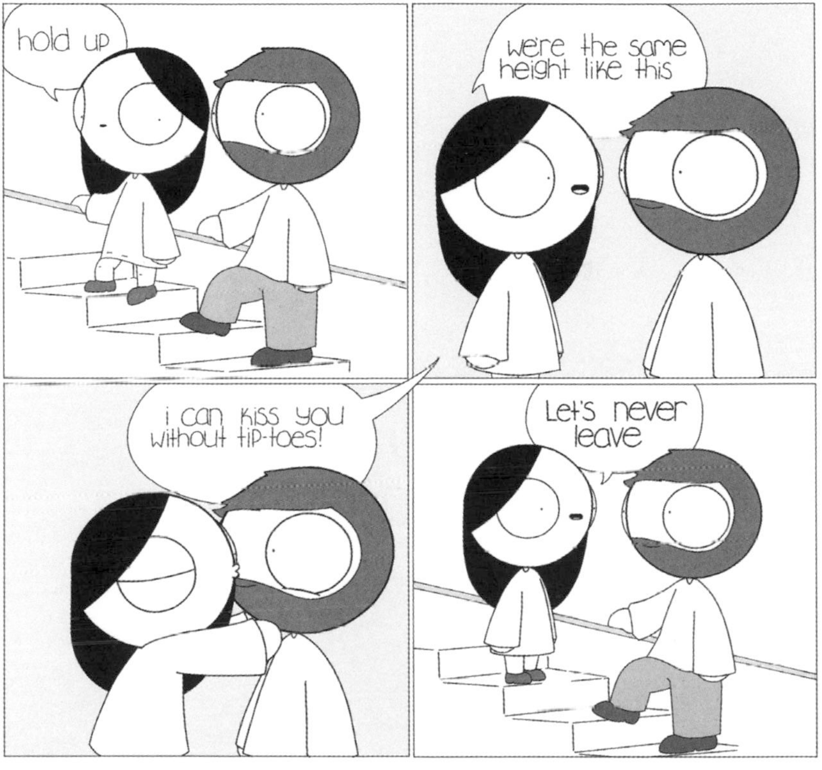
hold up
we're the same height like this
i can kiss you without tip-toes!
Let's never leave

His Shower vs. My Shower

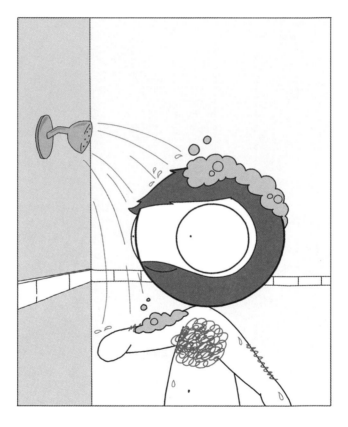

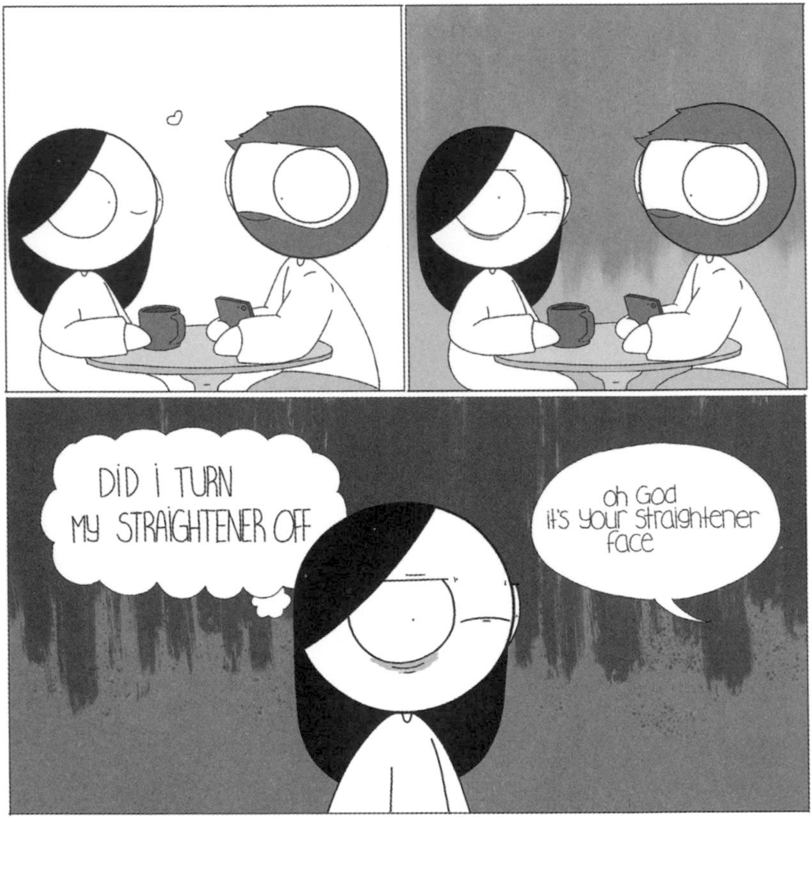
DID I TURN MY STRAIGHTENER OFF
oh God it's your straightener face

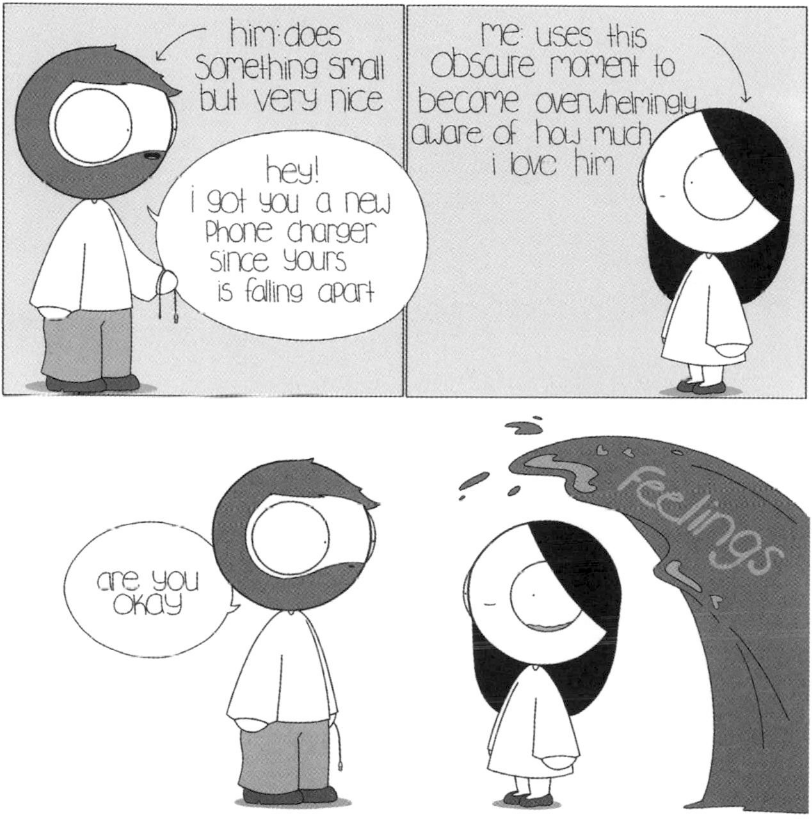
him: does something small but very nice
hey! i got you a new phone charger since yours is falling apart
me: uses this obscure moment to become overwhelmingly aware of how much i love him
are you okay
feelings

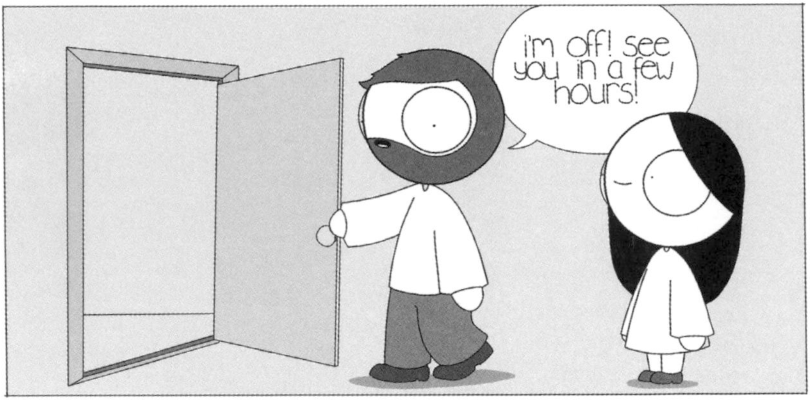
i'm off! see you in a few hours!

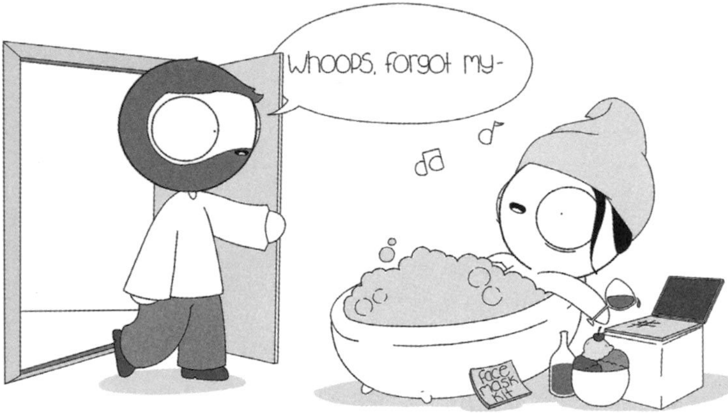
Whoops, forgot my-
face mask kit

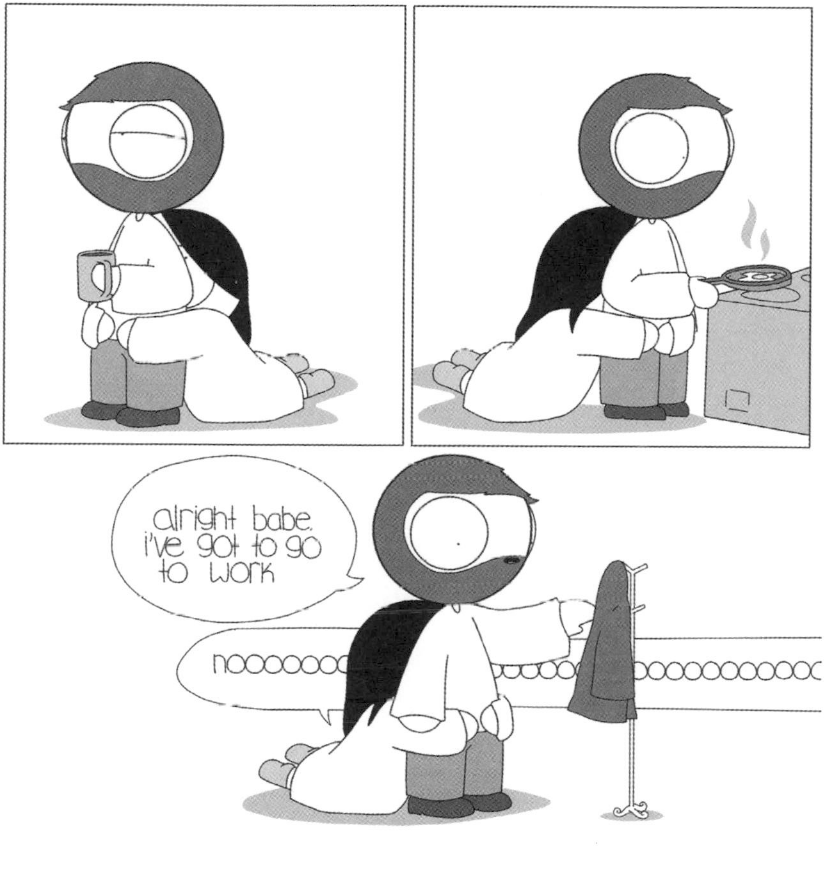
alright babe. i've got to go to work
noooooooooooooooooooooooooooooo

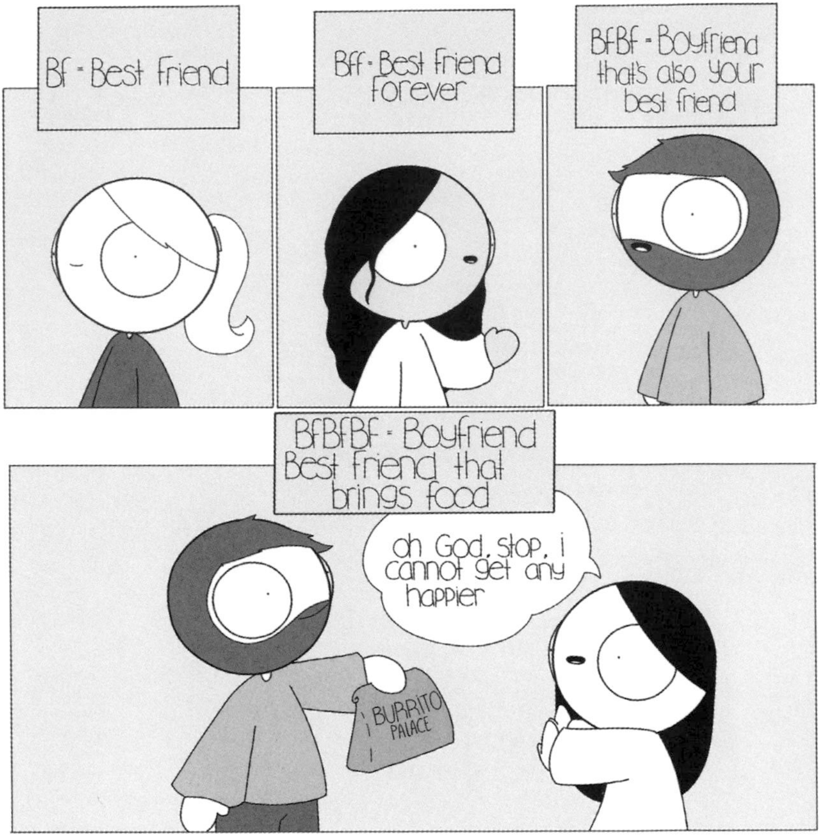
Bf = Best friend
Bff = Best friend forever
BfBf = Boyfriend that's also your best friend
BfBfBf = Boyfriend Best friend that brings food
oh God, stop, i cannot get any happier
BURRITO PALACE

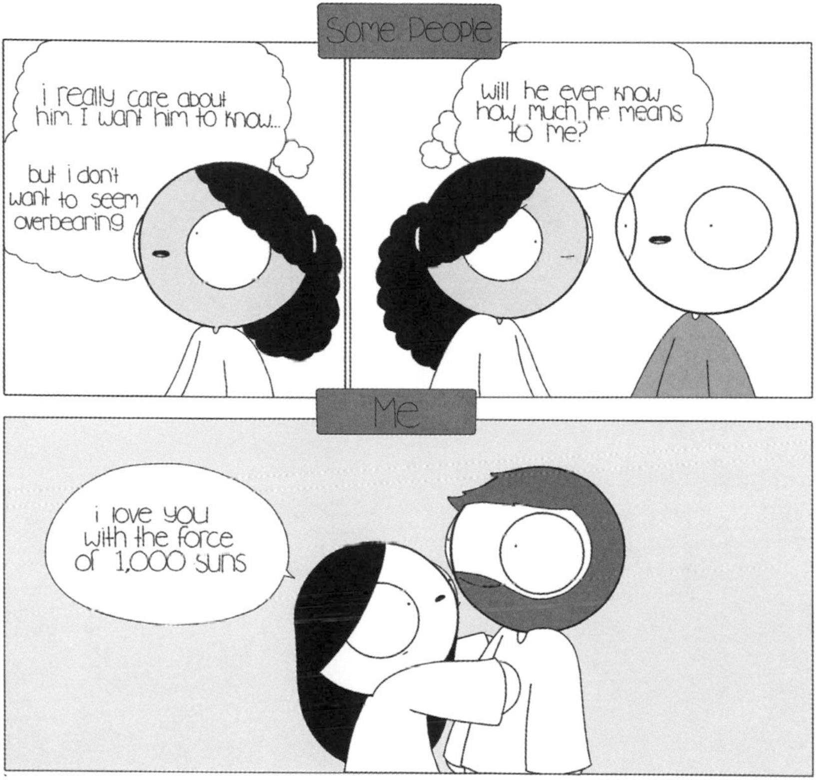
Some People
i really care about him. I want him to know...
but i don't want to seem overbearing
will he ever know how much he means to me?
Me
i love you with the force of 1,000 suns

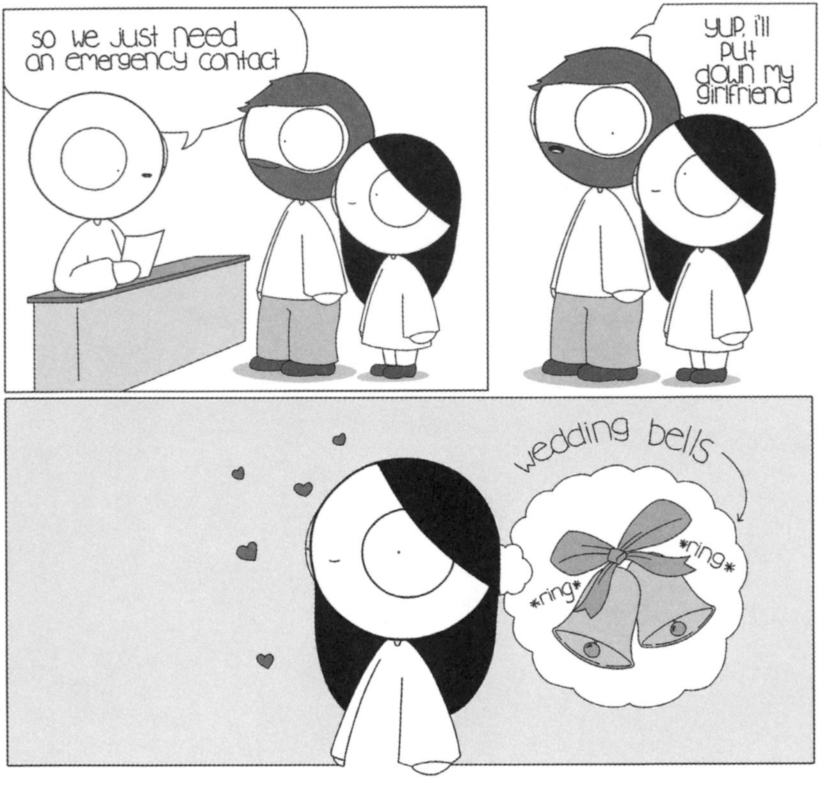
so we just need an emergency contact
yup, i'll put down my girlfriend
wedding bells
ring
ring

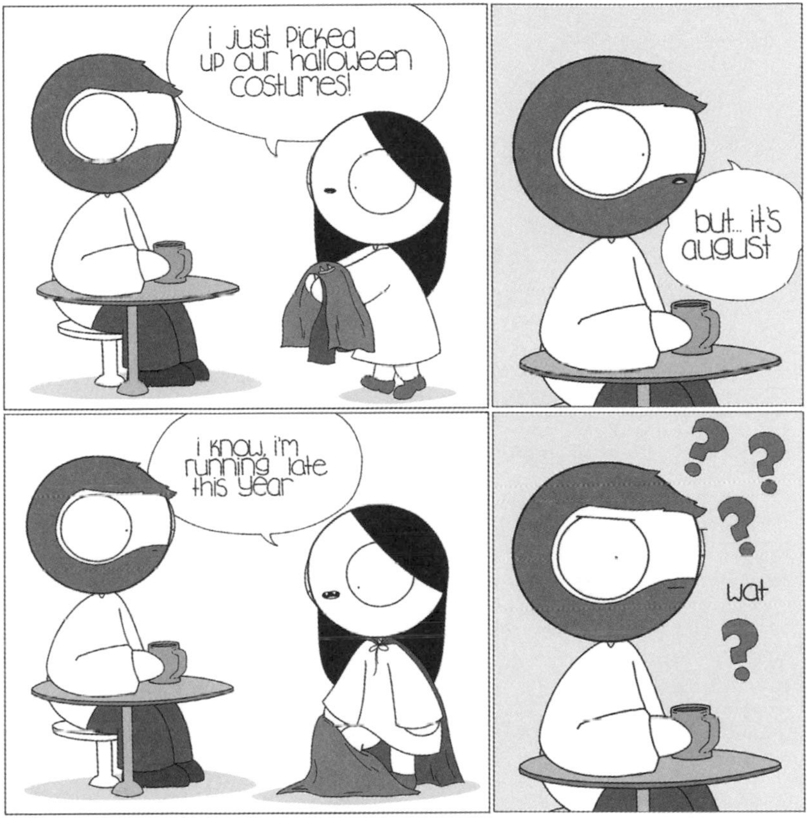
i just picked up our halloween costumes!
but... it's august
i know, i'm running late this year
wat

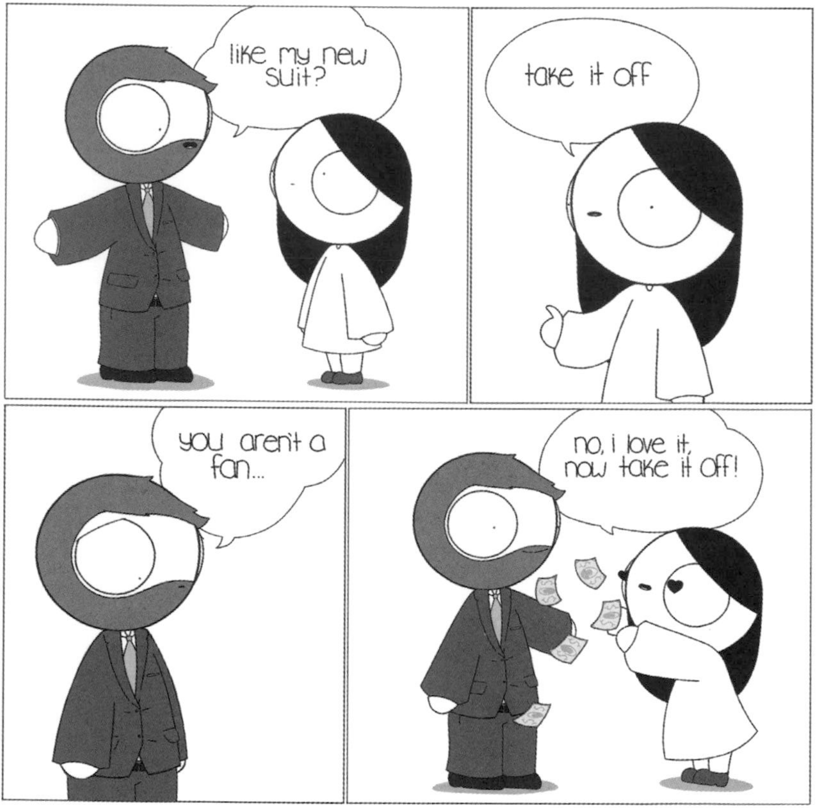
like my new suit?
take it off
you aren't a fan...
no, i love it, now take it off!

Morning Awakeness

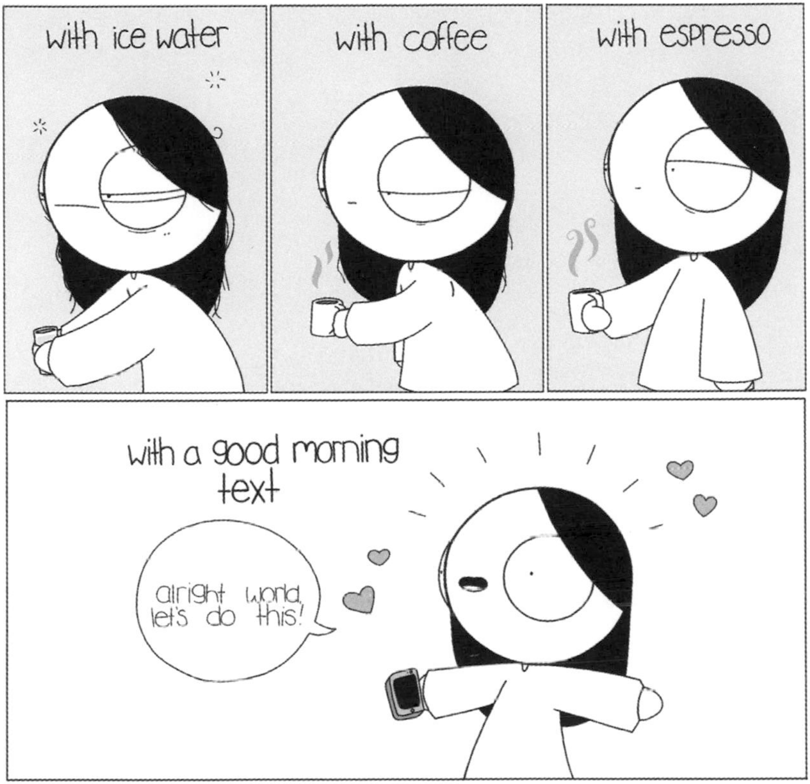
with ice water
with coffee
with espresso
with a good morning text
alright world, let's do this!

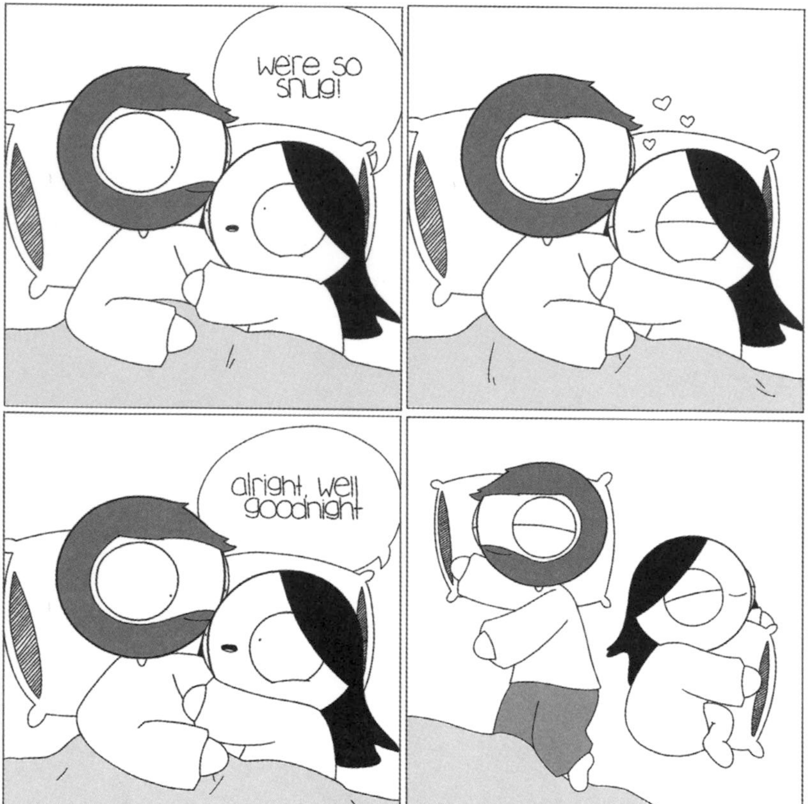
we're so snug!
alright, well goodnight

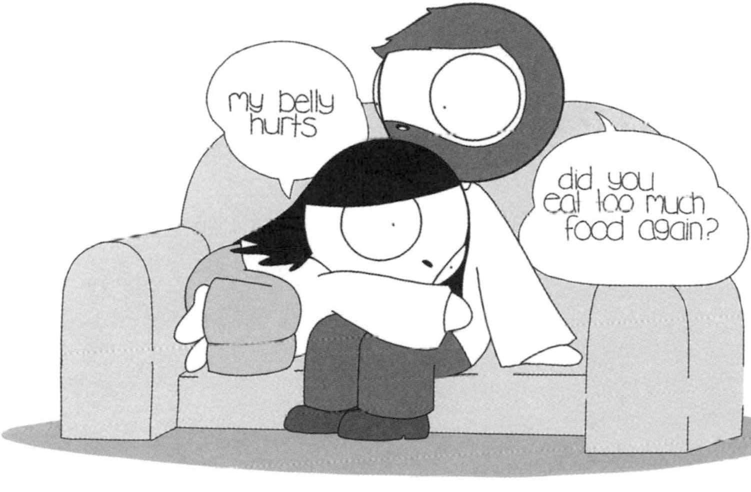
my belly hurts
did you eat too much food again?

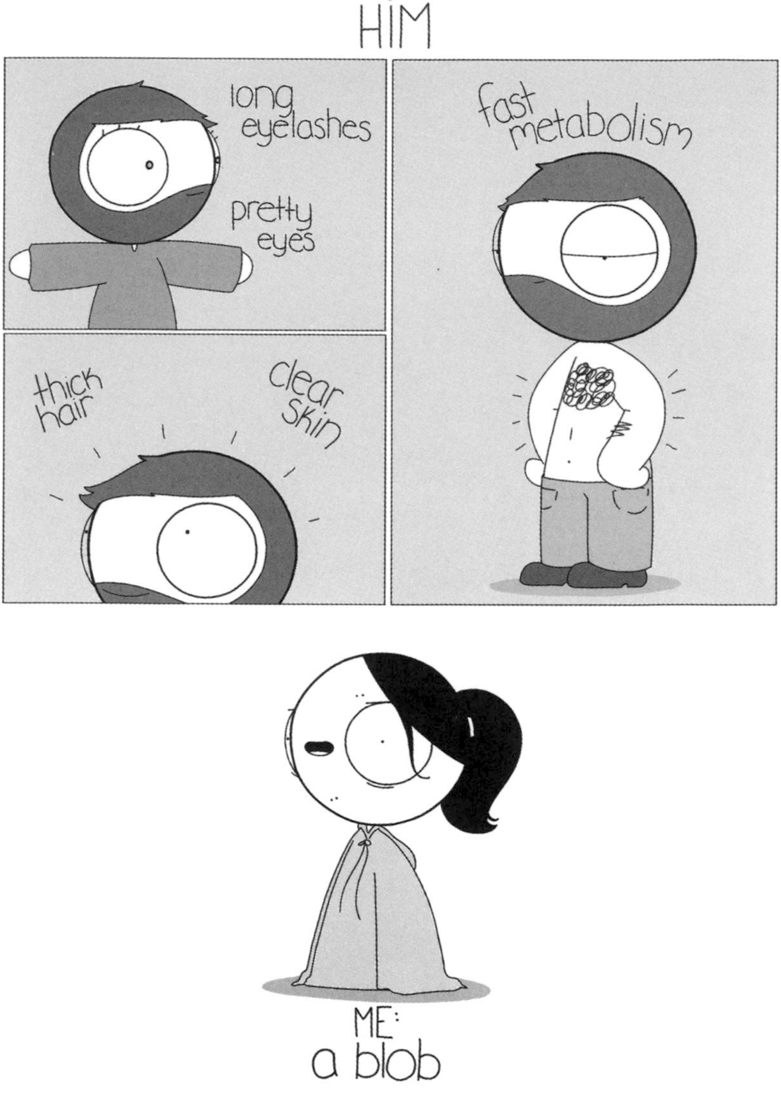
HIM
long eyelashes
pretty eyes
fast metabolism
thick hair
clear skin
ME:
a blob

There Are Two Types Of People...

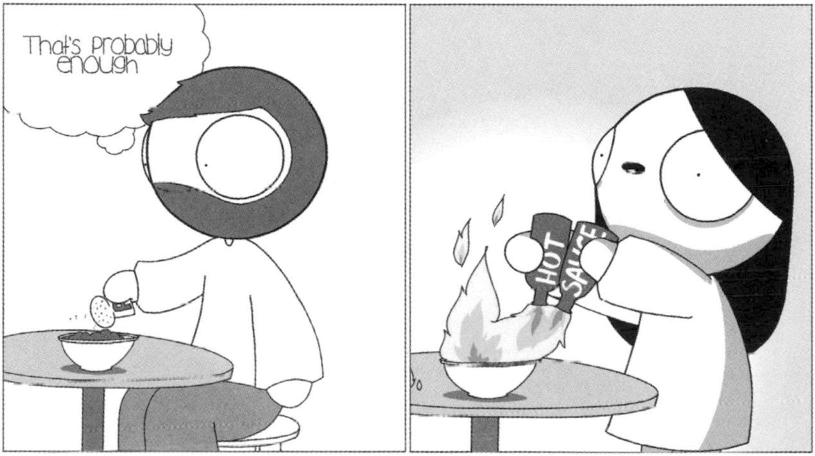
That's probably enough
HOT
SAUCE!

Wednesdays

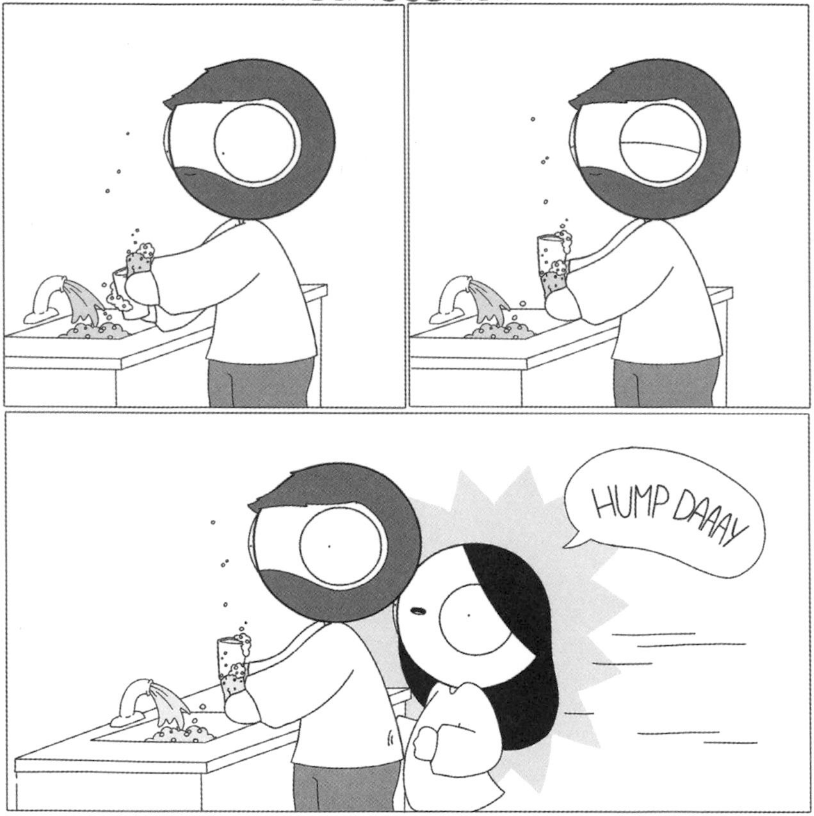
HUMP DAAAY

Best Ways To Stay Warm

bundle up
Start a fire!
have a hot drink
Hold on to your shirtless boyfriend's back
Please don't get dressed yet

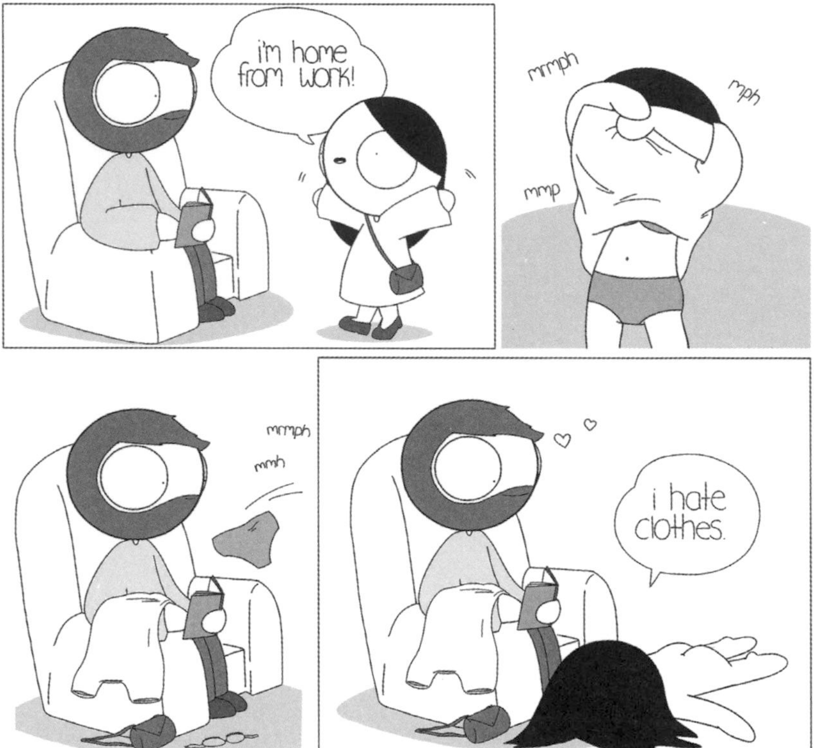
i'm home from work!
mrmph
mph
mmp
mrmph
mmh
i hate clothes.

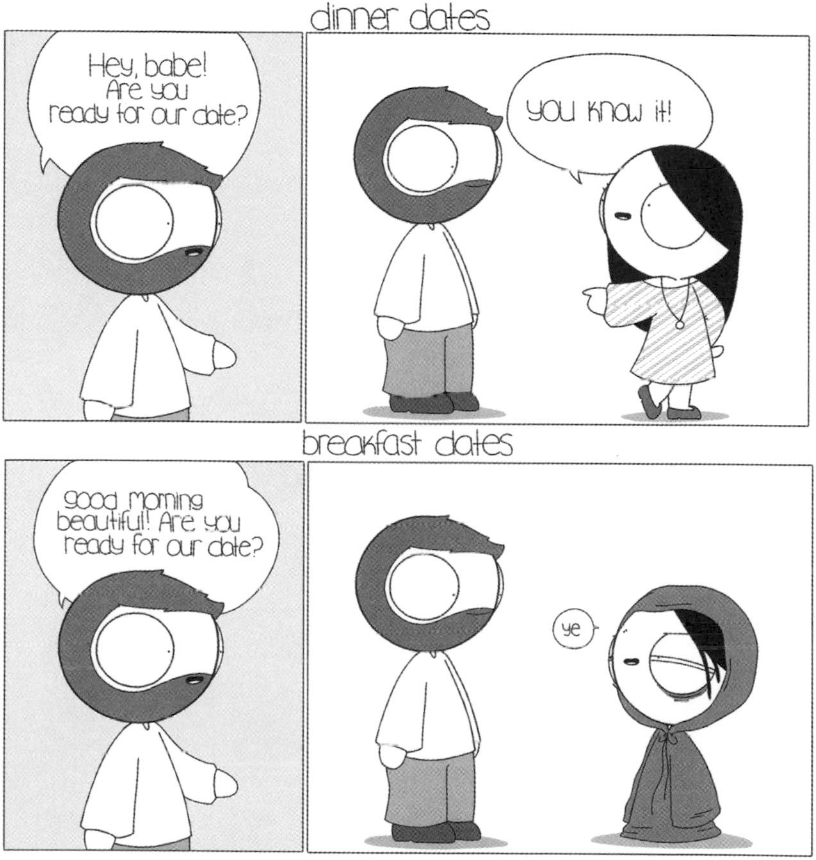
dinner dates
Hey, babe! Are you ready for our date?
you know it!
breakfast dates
good morning beautiful! Are you ready for our date?
ye

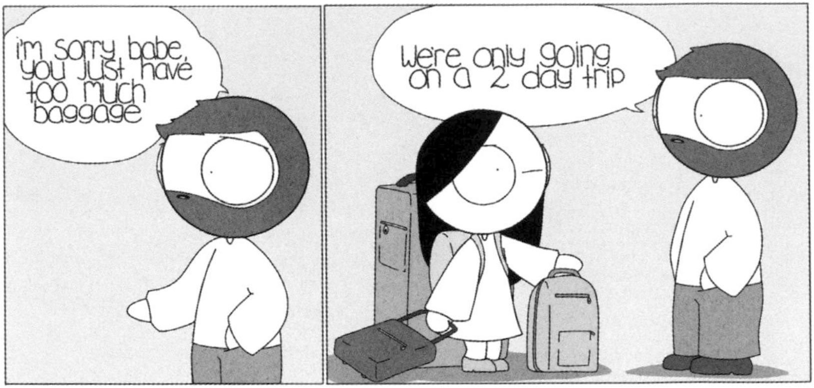
i'm sorry babe, you just have too much baggage
We're only going on a 2 day trip

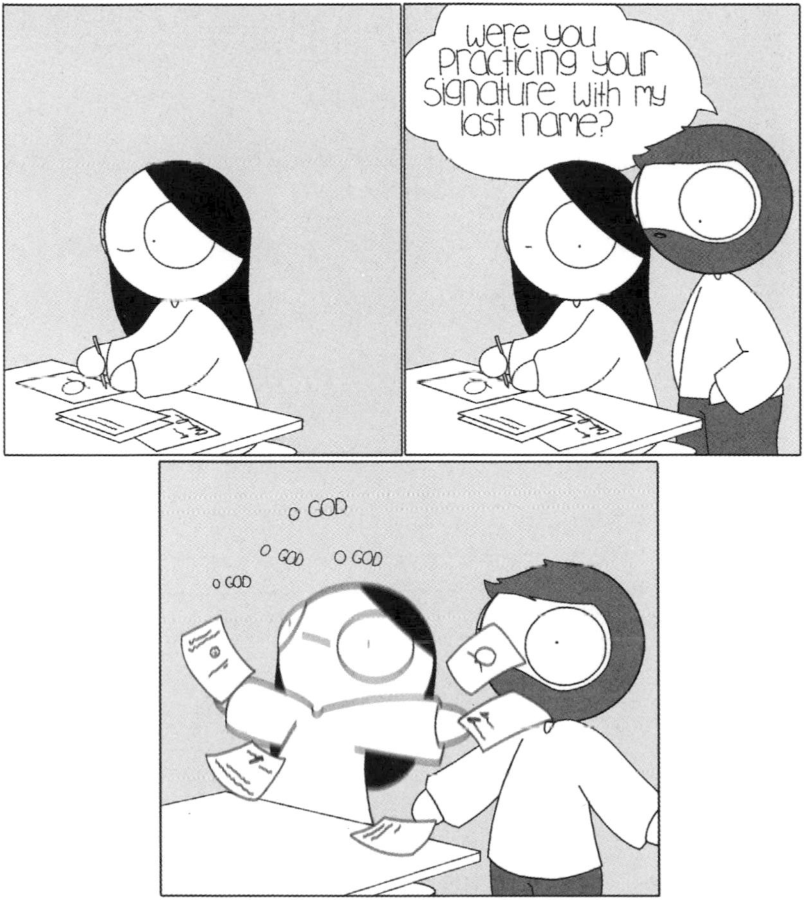
were you practicing your signature with my last name?
o GOD
o GOD
o GOD
o GOD

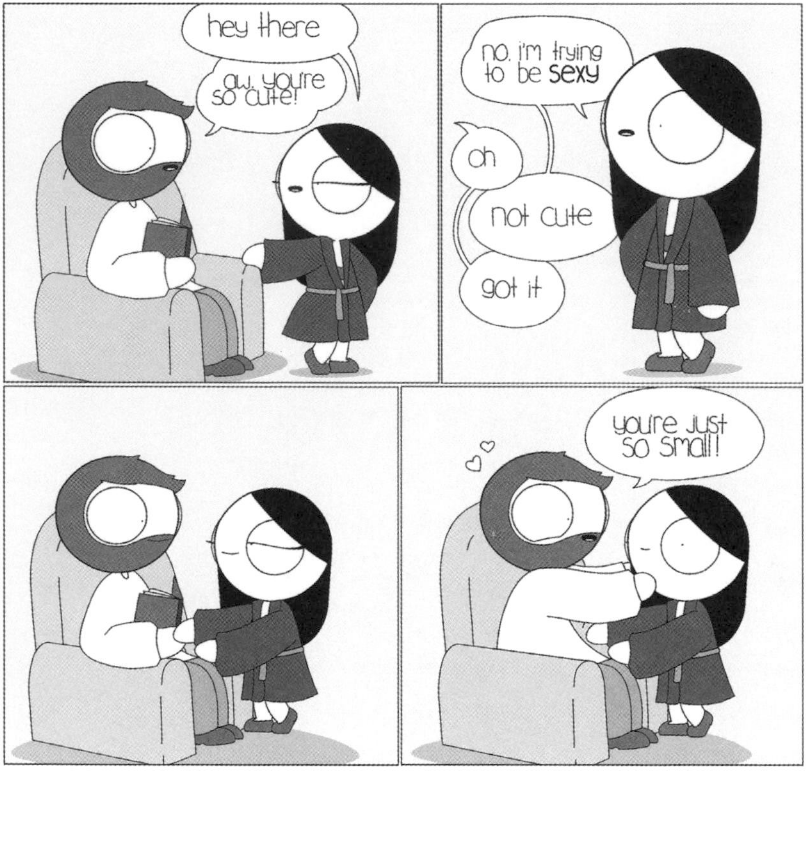
hey there
aw, you're so cute!
no, i'm trying to be sexy
oh
not cute
got it
you're just so small!

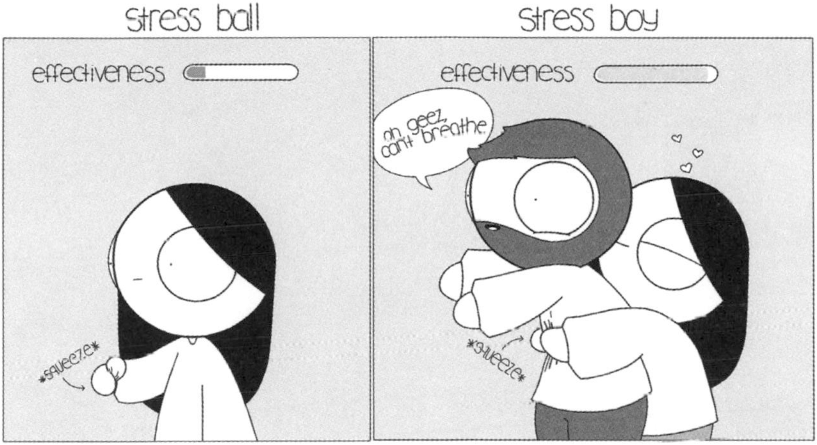
stress ball
effectiveness
squeeze
stress boy
effectiveness
oh geez, can't breathe
squeeze

Step 1: make room nice & cold
Step 2: gather blankets
it's freezing!
good!

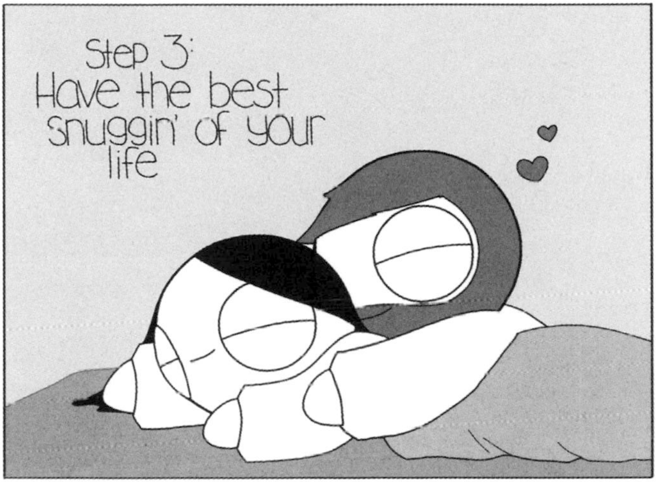
Step 3:
Have the best
snuggin' of your
life

Selfie Expectation

Selfie Reality

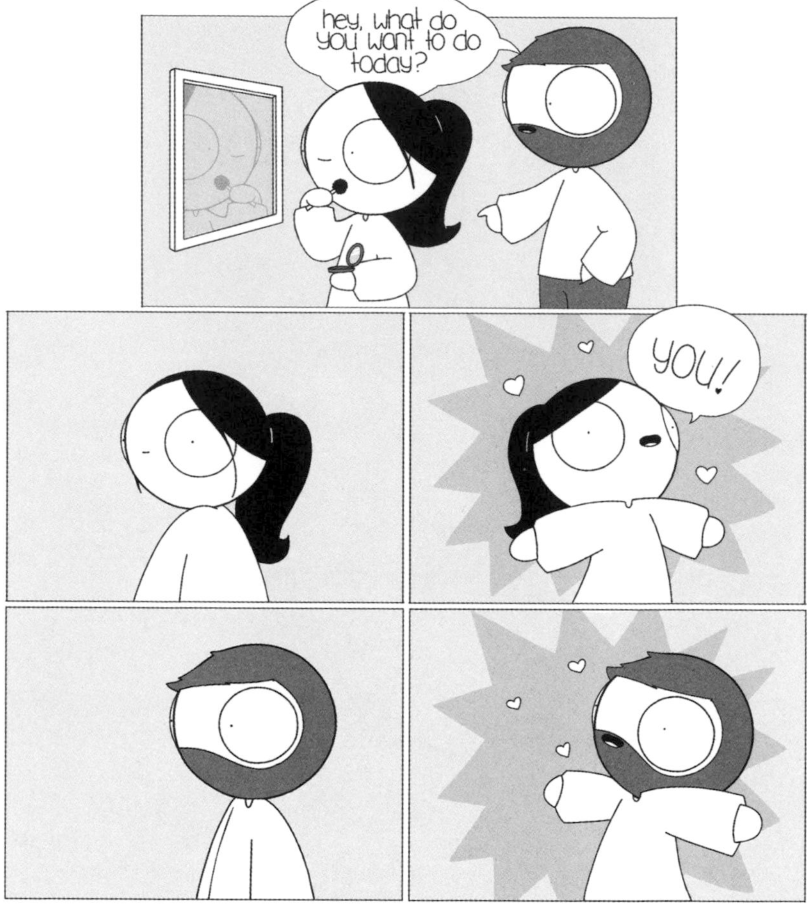
hey, what do you want to do today?
YOU!

a night alone - expectation

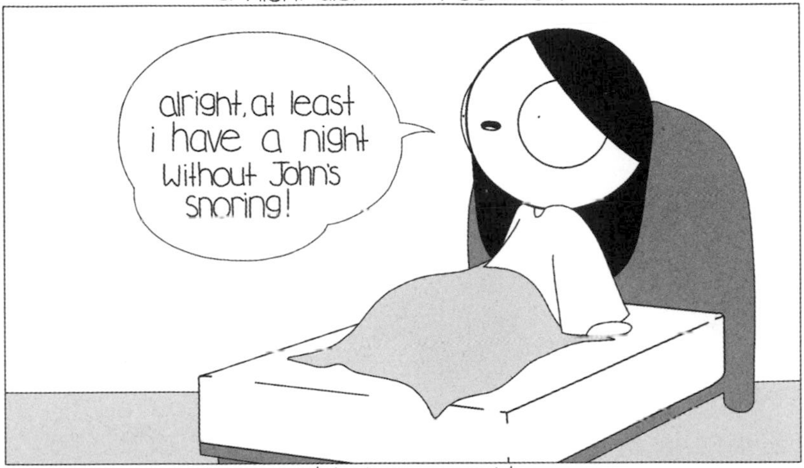
alright, at least i have a night without John's snoring!

a night alone - reality

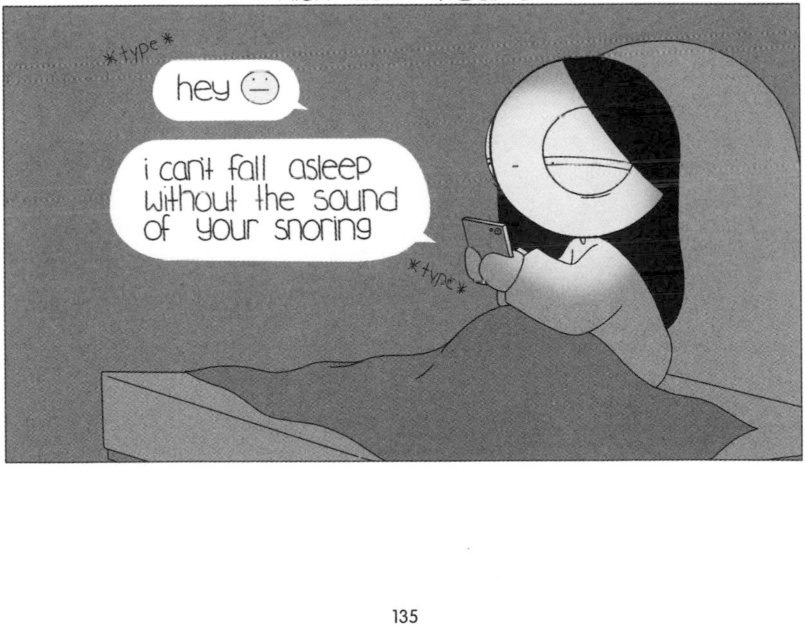
type
hey 😐
i can't fall asleep without the sound of your snoring
type

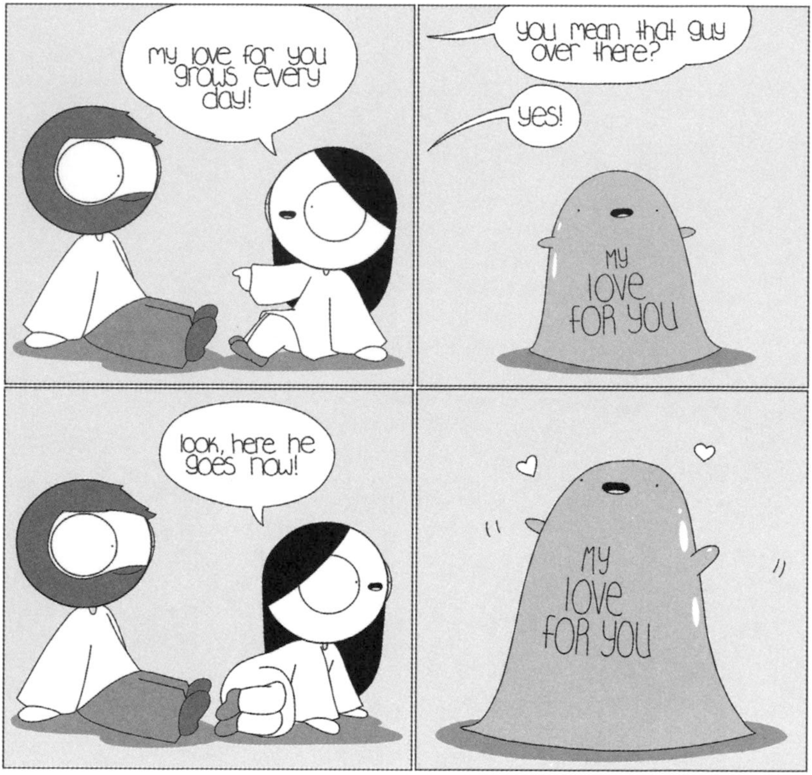
my love for you grows every day!
you mean that guy over there?
yes!
MY love FOR YOU
look, here he goes now!
MY love FOR YOU

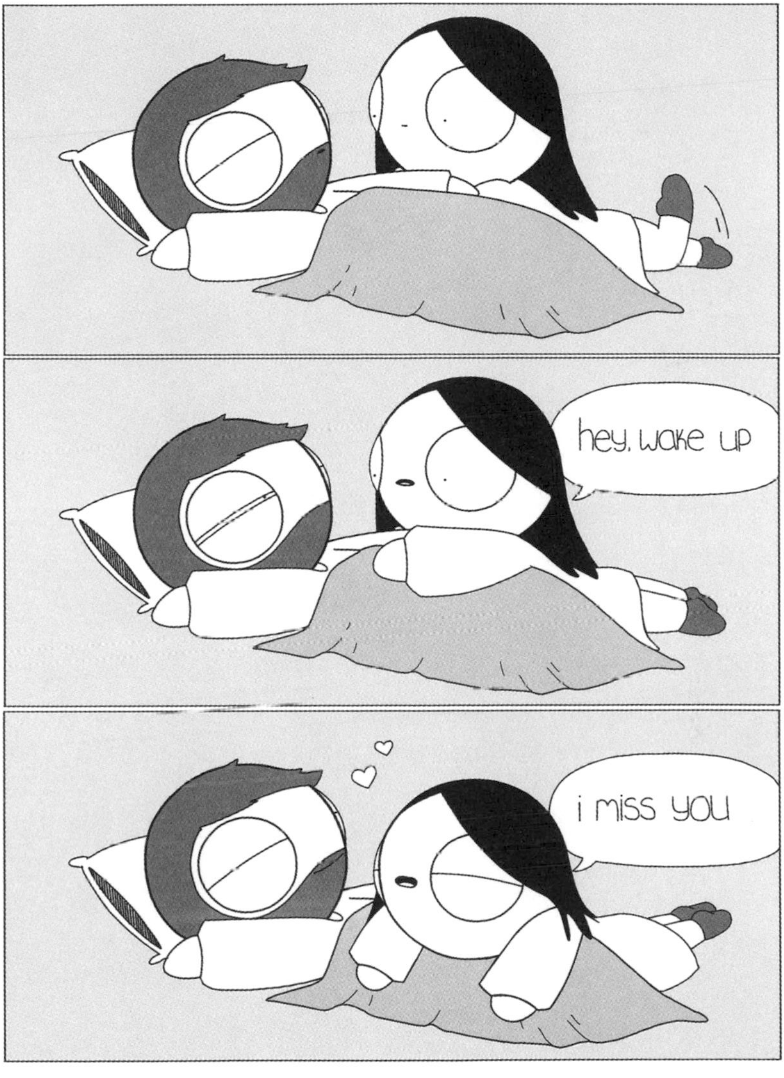
hey, wake up
i miss you

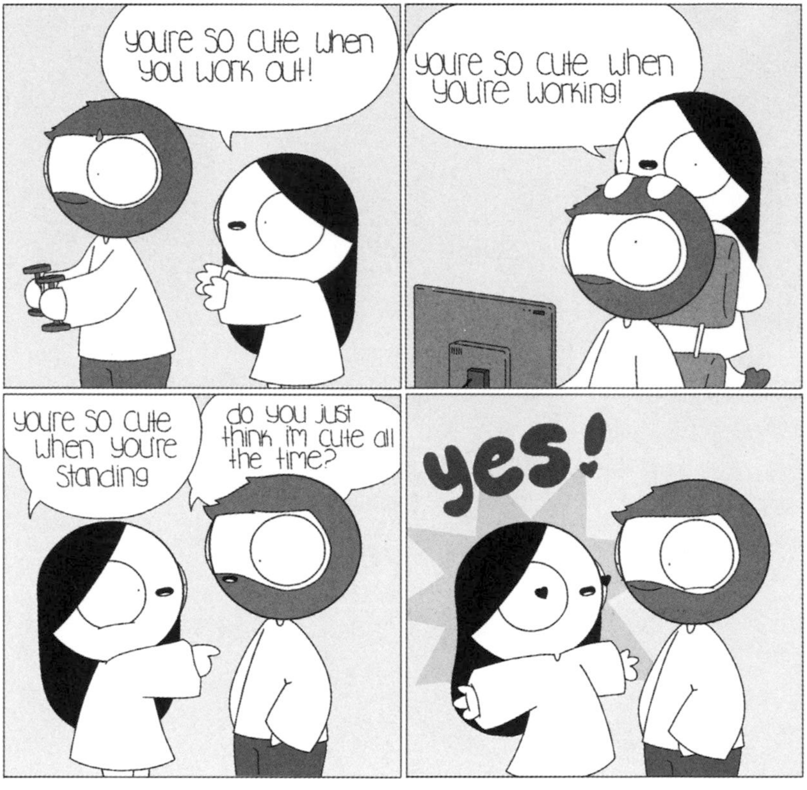
you're so cute when you work out!
you're so cute when you're working!
you're so cute when you're standing
do you just think i'm cute all the time?
yes!

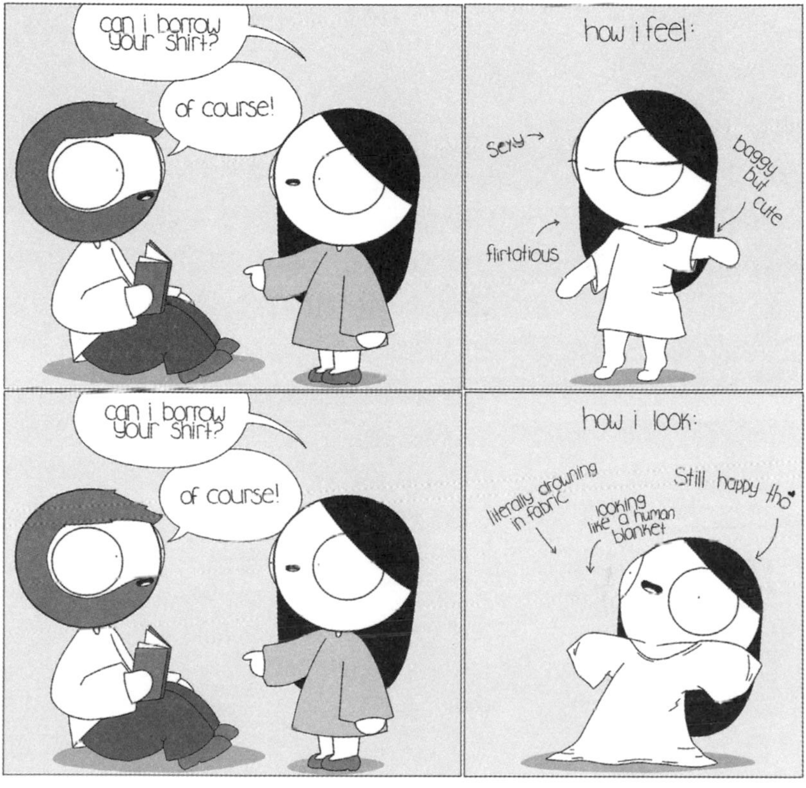
can i borrow your shirt?
of course!
how i feel:
sexy
baggy but cute
flirtatious
can i borrow your shirt?
of course!
how i look:
literally drowning in fabric
looking like a human blanket
still happy tho

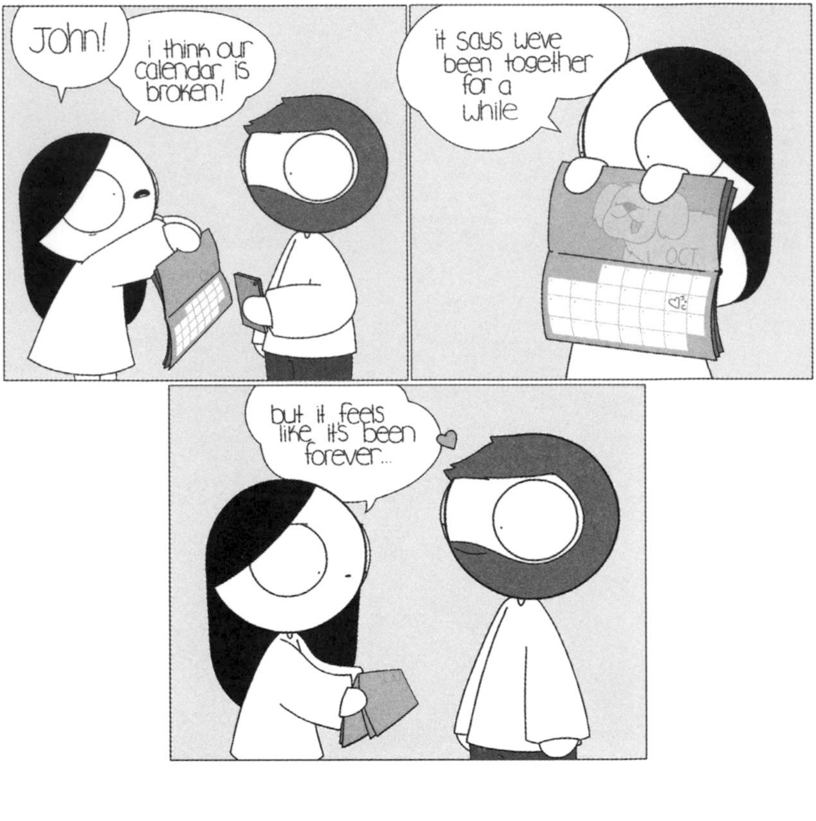
John!
i think our calendar is broken!
it says weve been together for a while
OCT.
but it feels like it's been forever...

Ways To Show Your Boyfriend Your Appreciation

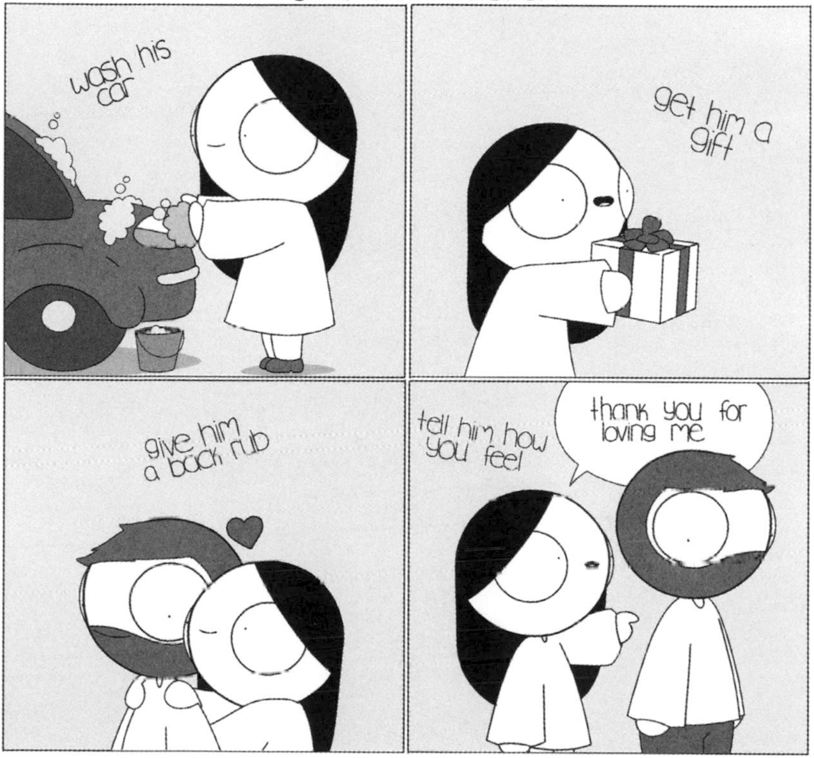

wash his car
get him a gift
give him a back rub
tell him how you feel
thank you for loving me

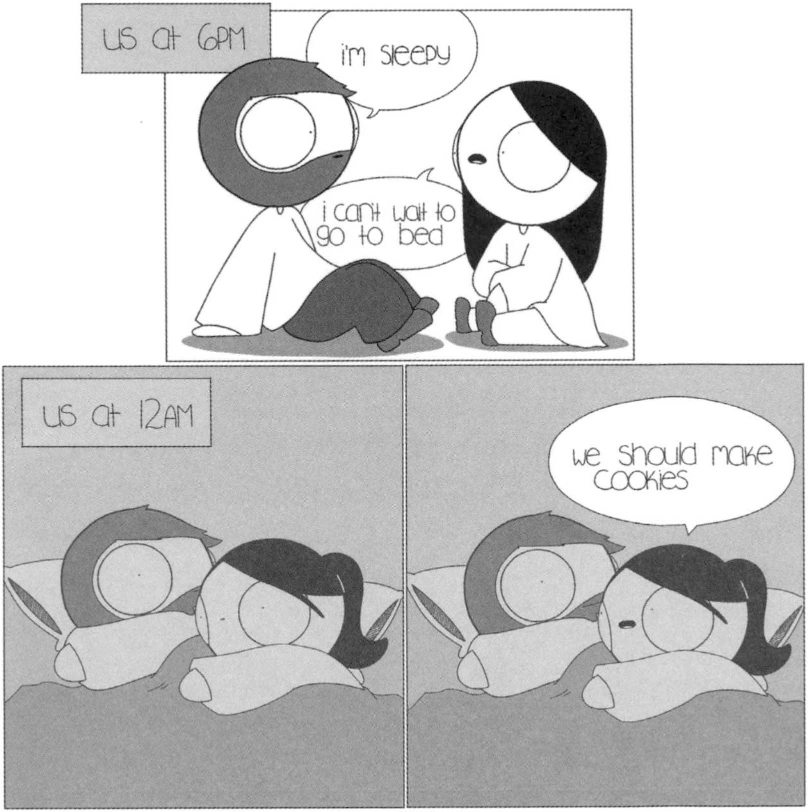

us at 6PM
i'm sleepy
i can't wait to go to bed
us at 12AM
we should make cookies

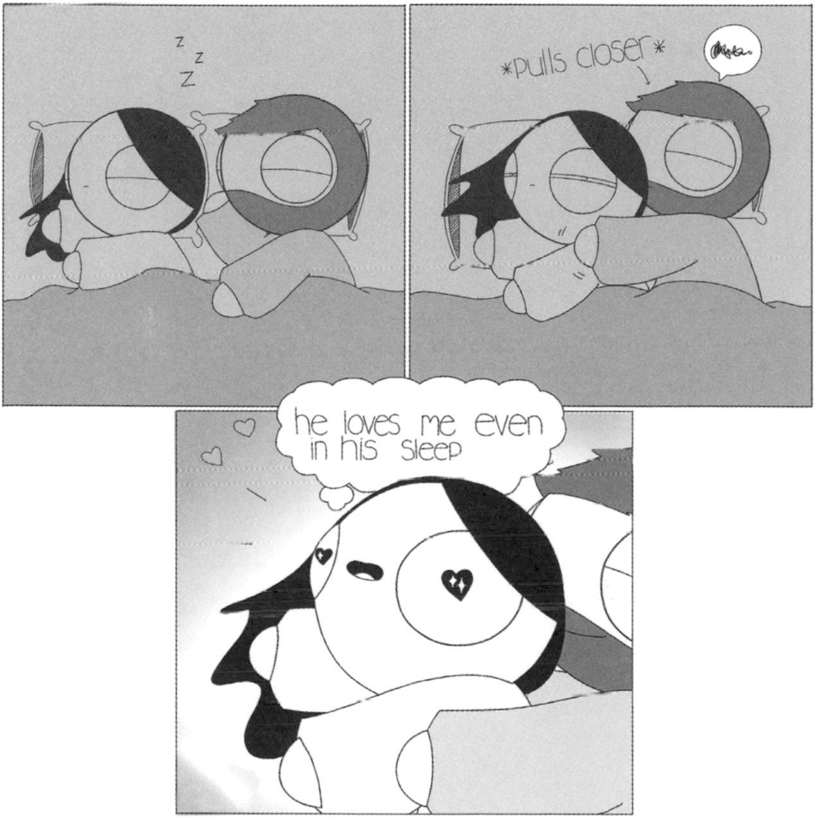
z z Z
pulls closer
he loves me even in his sleep

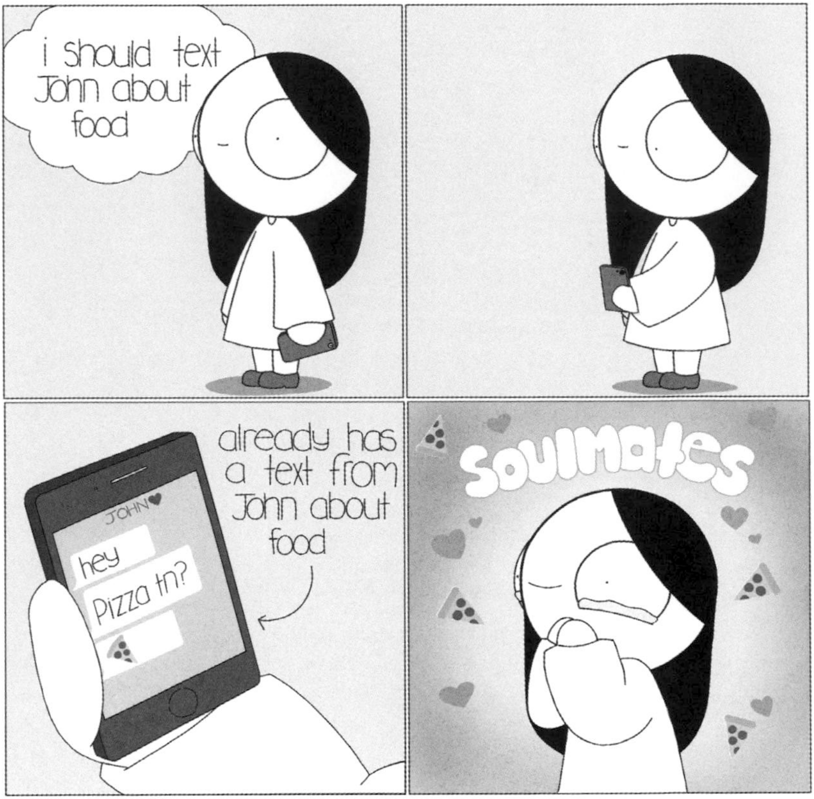
i should text John about food
already has a text from John about food
JOHN
hey
Pizza tn?
soulmates

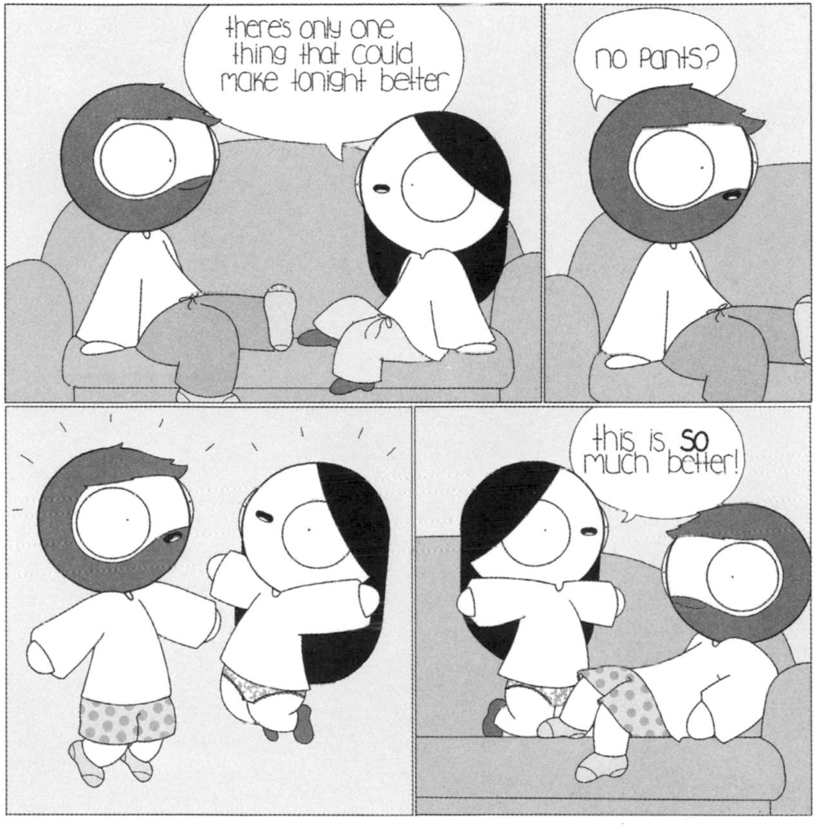
there's only one thing that could make tonight better
no pants?
this is SO much better!

Long Day

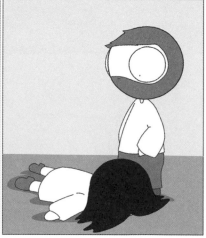

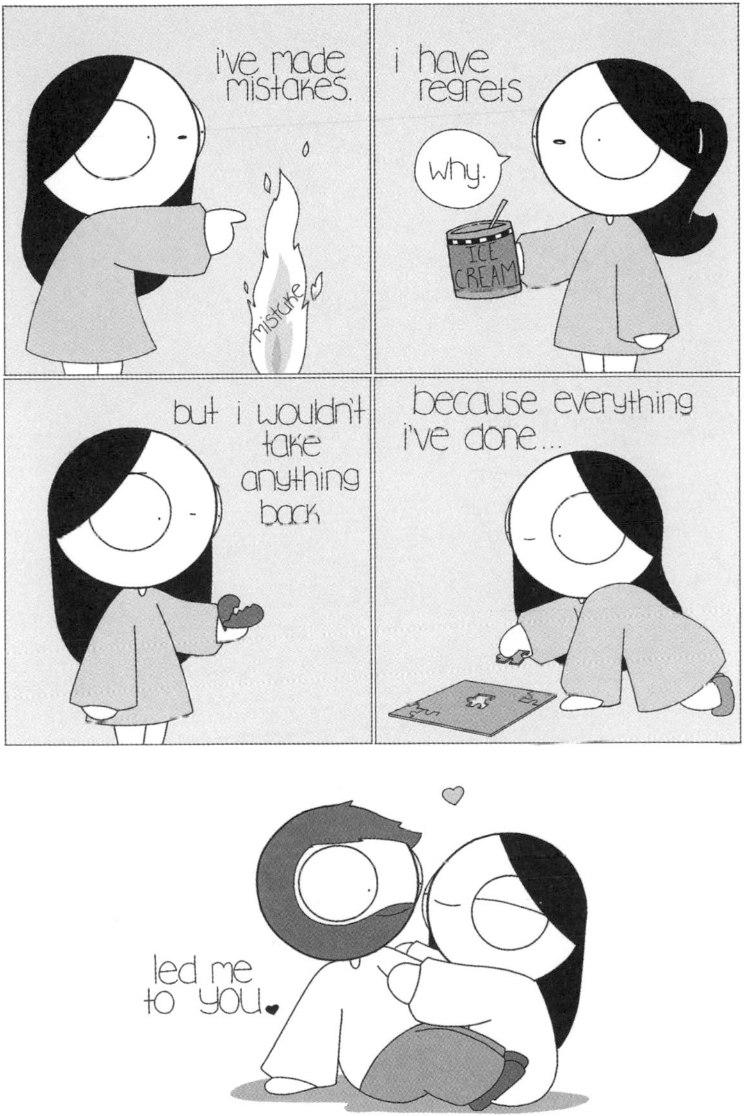
i've made mistakes.
mistake
i have regrets
why.
ICE CREAM
but i wouldn't take anything back
because everything i've done...
led me to you.

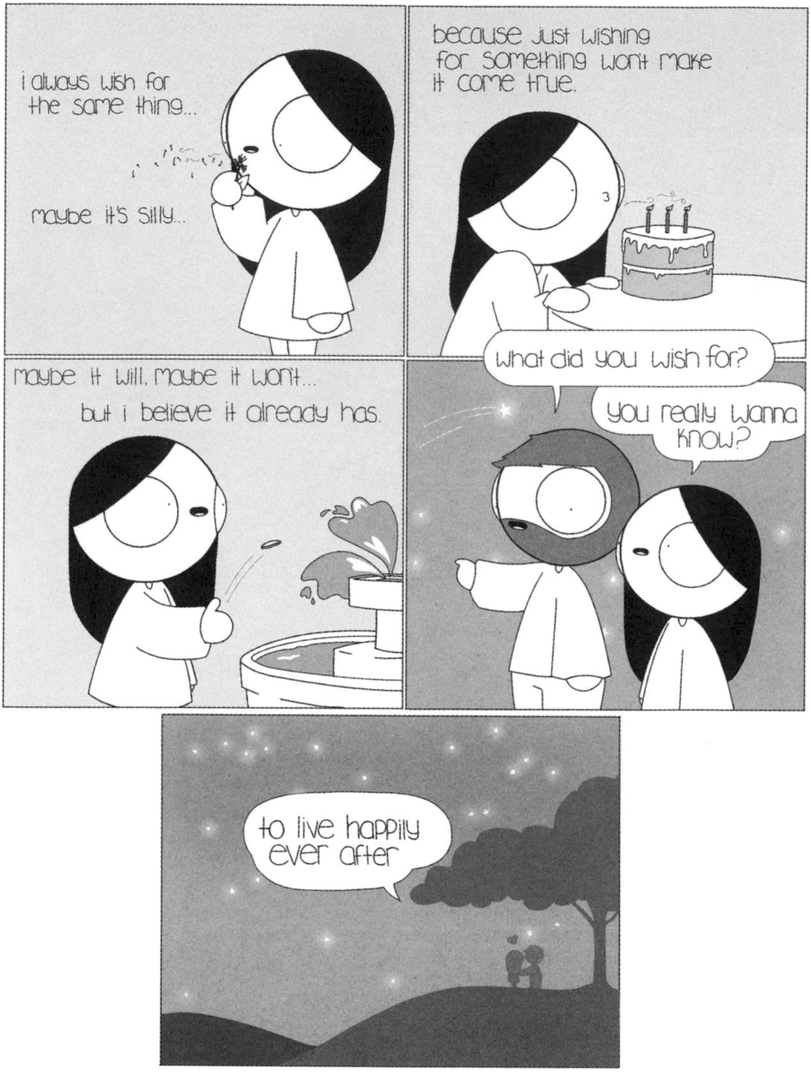
i always wish for the same thing...
maybe it's silly...
because just wishing for something won't make it come true.
maybe it will. maybe it won't...
but i believe it already has.
What did you wish for?
You really wanna know?
to live happily ever after

Catana Chetwynd is a self-taught traditional artist and the enthusiastic author of Catana Comics. She grew up in Saratoga Springs, New York, where she spent her time creating art and pursuing an education in psychology until accidentally stumbling into the world of comics. Not only is her boyfriend, John, the daily inspiration for her drawings, but he was also the one who suggested a comic series about their relationship in the first place. Thanks to his idea and his inspiring daily antics, Catana was able to pursue her childhood dream of being a cartoonist. She currently lives in New York with John, and their tiny, angry dog, Murph.

Andrews McMeel Publishing
a division of Andrews McMeel Universal
1130 Walnut Street, Kansas City, Missouri 64106

www.andrewsmcmeel.com

18 19 20 21 22 SDB 10 9 8 7 6 5 4 3 2 1

ISBN: 978-1-4494-9297-7

Library of Congress Control Number: 2017917515

Editor: Patty Rice
Art Director: Holly Swayne
Production Editor: David Shaw
Production Manager: Tamara Haus

ATTENTION: SCHOOLS AND BUSINESSES
Andrews McMeel books are available at quantity
discounts with bulk purchase for educational, business, or
sales promotional use. For information, please e-mail the
Andrews McMeel Publishing Special Sales Department:
specialsales@amuniversal.com.